YORK NOTES

General Editors: Professor A.N. Jeffares (*University of Stirling*) & Professor Suheil Bushrui (*American University of Beirut*)

Alfred, Lord Tennyson

SELECTED POEMS

Notes by Alastair Thomson

MA (EDINBURGH)
Professor of English,
The New University of Ulster

821·8

KC 8904450

 LONGMAN

YORK PRESS
Immeuble Esseily, Place Riad Solh, Beirut.

LONGMAN GROUP LIMITED
Longman House,
Burnt Mill,
Harlow,
Essex

First published 1984
ISBN 0 582 79213 4
Printed in Hong Kong by
Wilture Printing Co Ltd.

Contents

Part 1

Introduction

Life of Tennyson

Alfred, Lord Tennyson, was born in 1809 at Somersby, Lincolnshire, and died in 1892 at his summer home in Sussex. He was the fourth son of the Reverend George Clayton Tennyson and his wife Elizabeth, after George, who had died in infancy, Frederick (1807), and Charles (1808). The poet's grandfather, George Tennyson the elder, was a solicitor who established himself as a substantial landowner. He was an unstable man, subject to violent rages and self-pity, and something of a domestic tyrant. His first-born son, George Clayton, the father of Alfred Tennyson, inherited many of his failings, without his talent for business, and throughout his life remained turbulent and lonely, and always liable to fits of black depression. Disappointed in him, his father passed him over in favour of his younger son Charles, who inherited the bulk of the family fortune, on the death of George Tennyson in 1835. George Clayton Tennyson had died four years earlier; his son Alfred probably inherited at least £6,000, and although he consistently worried about money, and would speak of himself as a poor man, he was comfortably off for most of his life, despite his losses in the early 1840s as a result of bad investment, and indeed left £57,000, most of it from poetry. Charles Tennyson added the ancient name of d'Eyncourt to his own. The almost inevitable quarrel between the Tennysons of Somersby Rectory (eleven sons and daughters) and the crested and pedigreed Tennyson d'Eyncourts of Bayons Manor, extended and made spectacularly medieval in keeping with Charles Tennyson d'Eyncourt's ambitions, continued for many years. Although George Clayton and Charles Tennyson d'Eyncourt did not quarrel, the Somersby Tennysons mocked the pretensions of the Tennyson d'Eyncourts, who thought them uncouth, and some of whom were later angered by Tennyson's fame, and by his elevation to the peerage. The difficulties of life with his father were a formative experience for Alfred. His mother was sweet-tempered, but his father's depressions and nervous disorders strongly affected his large family. He drank heavily, and behaved violently. Tennyson's brother Frederick, who was as wayward and violent as his father, said that if they had not been living in a civilised country they would have murdered each other. His other brothers all had difficulty in coping with life. Charles (the Charles Tennyson Turner of the charming

sonnet, 'Letty's Globe') was addicted for years to opium; Edward
spent most of his life in an asylum; Arthur suffered from alcoholism,
Septimus from nervous depression. To the end of his days Alfred was
affected by shyness and morbid depressions, and for years believed
that he had inherited epilepsy from his father.

His unpublished juvenilia include the visionary 'Armageddon', and
the drama 'The Devil and the Lady', both unfinished. He published his
first volume in 1827 (*Poems by Two Brothers*, mainly by Charles and
Alfred, with a few pieces by Frederick), and in the same year entered
Trinity College, Cambridge. At Cambridge he met Arthur Henry
Hallam, the great friend of his youth. Cambridge itself meant little to
him; in later life he said there was a lack of love in the place. Although
he was a valued member of the Apostles, a brilliant undergraduate
debating society, at whose meetings he rarely spoke, and although he
won the Chancellor's Gold Medal with his poem 'Timbuctoo', he left
Cambridge in 1831 without regrets, and without a degree. The year
before he had carried money and secret messages with Arthur Hallam
to the Spanish insurrectionary Constitutionalists, in whose cause the
Apostles were interested. His 1830 volume, *Poems, Chiefly Lyrical*,
had been severely handled by the critic John Wilson in *Blackwood's
Magazine*; *Poems*, of 1832, was harshly reviewed by Croker in the no
less influential *Quarterly Review*. The greatest sorrow Tennyson ever
knew was the death of Hallam in 1833. Some of his finest poetry was
written then, and the earliest of the one hundred and thirty-three lyric
sections of *In Memoriam A.H.H.* date from this period.

The two-volume *Poems* of 1842, which included revisions of some of
the earlier work, established his reputation with the poetry-reading
public. Five years later he published *The Princess*, a 'medley', as he
called it, or playful satire on the contemporary question of women's
rights and education. With *In Memoriam* of 1850, which he had been
writing at intervals since Hallam's death, his fame as the greatest living
English poet was assured. In the same year he succeeded Wordsworth
as Poet Laureate, and married Emily Sellwood, by whom he had two
sons, Hallam and Lionel. The brilliant monodrama *Maud* was published in 1855, and four *Idylls of the King* in 1859. Tennyson became a
public figure, pestered by visiting admirers, though remaining shy and
acutely sensitive to criticism. 'Enoch Arden' of 1864 helped to establish
his fame in Europe. The *Idylls of the King*, in twelve books, was finally
completed in 1874. In 1883 he became Baron Tennyson of Aldworth
and Freshwater. The plays which he wrote in his later years have no
particular interest other than their authorship. He died in 1892, and
was buried in Westminster Abbey.

The friendship with Hallam

Hallam's death in 1833 was probably the greatest emotional experience of Tennyson's life. The two men had met at Cambridge in 1829. Hallam was two years younger than Tennyson. Although he wrote poetry both in English and Italian (he was an ardent admirer of Dante), his predilections were for metaphysics and philosophy. Unlike Tennyson he was a brilliant debater and public speaker. In section 87 (LXXXVII) of *In Memoriam*, Tennyson describes his intellectual authority at the meetings of the Apostles, when his friends 'hung to hear / The rapt oration flowing free,' and 'saw / The God within him light his face'. His father, the Whig historian Henry Hallam, had encouraged his precocity. The statesman Gladstone had been his intimate friend at Eton, and many years later said that Hallam was the most brilliant man he had ever known.

At Cambridge Hallam had missed his Eton friends, who had gone to Oxford. Tennyson had also been lonely during his first year there, missing the society of his talented brothers and sisters, with whom he had lived happily at Somersby when his father's temper and health permitted. Partly as a result of this, they quickly became friends. They travelled together to the Pyrenees – Tennyson's 1861 poem, 'In the Valley of Cauteretz', describes his emotions at revisiting a place first seen so many years ago with Hallam – and to the Rhine. Although Tennyson was a poor correspondent, with Hallam as with anyone else, they saw each other frequently. Hallam often visited the Tennysons at Somersby, which he seems to have found a change from the rigorous mental discipline imposed on him by his father in London. At Somersby he fell in love with Tennyson's sister Emily, to whom he became engaged. It used to be said that Tennyson found in Hallam the emotional and mental stability that he badly needed. But though his grasp of philosophical abstractions and concepts was greater than his friend's, Hallam too had his fears of madness, and thoughts of suicide. It is likely that each found stability in the other. Tennyson said of him that he was as near perfection as mortal man could be, and in *In Memoriam* he makes his dead friend a type or example of the greater human race to come. He also said that Hallam looked up to him as he looked up to Hallam. While travelling with his father on the continent in 1833, Hallam died suddenly at Vienna, of apoplexy. Tennyson broke the news to his sister Emily. Although *In Memoriam* and, in a different way, 'Morte d'Arthur' testify to his great grief, and although he was later to say that his life then seemed shattered, and that he wanted to die, he bore up well before his friends and family. He did not attend Hallam's funeral.

Several critics have thought it necessary to take up a stand on whether or not the friendship was homosexual. There is nothing to suggest that it was. Hallam had had one or two sentimental affairs with women before he fell in love with Emily Tennyson. Tennyson's deep mistrust of physical love, evident in his poetry, is of no great relevance. Of the line 'Oh, wast thou with me, dearest, then' in section 122 (CXXII) of *In Memoriam* he remarked to James Knowles, 'If anybody thinks I ever called him "dearest" in his life they are much mistaken, for I never even called him "dear"'. The appeal to the spirit of the dead in section 93 (XCIII) to 'Descend, and touch, and enter' has been brought in evidence, but there is nothing in it, or in the draft reading 'touch me: wed me', to suggest anything more than what is sometimes hoped of spirits. That Shakespeare's sonnets are an important stylistic analogue to *In Memoriam*, and that Hallam's father had reservations about them, means very little. The question is, in any real sense, unimportant.

Tennyson and his times

Tennyson's life spanned the nineteenth century, the greatest age of national power and national prosperity that Britain had known. He was born four years after the battle of Trafalgar saved the country from French invasion, and died only eight years before the coming of the twentieth century. With the final defeat of Napoleon at Waterloo in 1815, Britain entered on a long period of relative peace, broken only by the Crimean War, when in 1854 she briefly allied herself with Turkey and France against Russia. Mistrust of France lingered, and flared up in 1851 at the time of the *coup d'état* of Louis Napoleon, when it seemed as if a clash was imminent. Tennyson fully shared this mistrust. He was much less of a cosmopolitan than Browning, in spite of his foreign and even exotic appearance, and tended to express strong racial prejudices about Britain's unruly neighbours, speaking of the Irish and French in *In Memoriam* in terms of 'the blind hysterics of the Celt' and 'the red fool-fury of the Seine', and characterising the French, in a call to arms written at the time of the *coup d'état*, as 'bearded monkeys of lust and blood'. He was strongly opposed to Gladstone's policy of Home Rule for Ireland, and on the whole believed in the civilising mission of British rule abroad, although he had few illusions about commercial enterprise.

During the century many attempts at political and social reform were made. It is true that one act of Parliament resulted in the intolerable system of workhouses for the poor. But the Reform Bills of 1832, 1867, and 1884 corrected some abuses, and ensured a wider representation. On the other hand, the industrial power that made Britain powerful was achieved at a terrible cost in human misery. She had been active in fighting the slave trade, but while slaves were freed overseas, industrial slaves were created at home. London was the largest and richest city in the world. It was also a city where the misery of the masses impoverished by the march of industry was everywhere apparent. It was in London that Karl Marx chose to settle, and to analyse the evils of a society in which men were little better than industrial units, or instruments of capital. Dickens, Ruskin, Carlyle, Kingsley, and Morris showed the estate of man in a modern industrial society. It is to Tennyson's credit that he did not close his eyes to it. In *Maud* he speaks bitterly of 'the golden age'.

> Peace sitting under her olive, and slurring the days gone by,
> When the poor are hovelled and hustled together, each sex, like swine,
> When only the ledger lives, and when only not all men lie;
> Peace in her vineyard — yes! — but a company forges the wine.

In 'Locksley Hall Sixty Years After' (1886), he answers the celebration of progress in his 'Locksley Hall' of the late 1830s.

> Is it well that while we range with Science, glorying in the Time,
> City children soak and blacken soul and sense in city slime? . . .

> There the smouldering fire of fever creeps across the rotted floor,
> And the crowded couch of incest in the warrens of the poor.

Yet in the same poem he speaks sardonically of 'the suffrage of the plow', and, remarking that 'the tonguesters' and the illiterate mob they flatter will cause Britain's ruin, offers mocking counsel.

> You that woo the Voices — tell them 'old experience is a fool,'
> Teach your flattered kings that only those who cannot read can
>   rule . . .

> Tumble Nature heel o'er head, and, yelling with the yelling street,
> Set the feet above the brain and swear the brain is in the feet.

Although he was sickened by the lot of the industrial age's poor, he was not a democrat. His call in *Maud*, indistinguishable from the voice of his hero, is not for the people to take up arms, but for a strong man who can rule, and save the country from such a despot as France's Louis Napoleon, or from the power of the mob. It should be remembered that although William Morris was a Communist, and Ruskin evolved for himself at one stage a peculiar kind of Tory communism, the greatest writers of the century, while condemning the exploitation of the labouring classes, did not adhere to any doctrine of egalitarianism. Nor had Britain experienced anything comparable to the widespread European revolts of 1848. The Chartist movement, which demanded honourable terms for the workers, lost its momentum and died. Its natural successor was the Trades Union movement. This too had had its martyrs; in 1834 several labourers, known as the Tolpuddle Martyrs, were transported for joining a trade union illegally. But on the whole the working classes were more concerned with the improvement of conditions, than with political theory, or the founding of a socialist state.

It should also be remembered that the collapse of the French Revolution into anarchy and despotism had profoundly affected many people's thinking about methods of change. William Wordsworth (1770–1850) and P.B. Shelley (1793–1822) rightly saw the reasons for these excesses in the outrages which had inspired the Revolution. In a striking image in *The Prelude*, Wordsworth describes the Terror as the deluge following the breaking of a huge reservoir of guilt, filled up from age to age, which now spread its loathsome charge through the land. Shelley looked forward to a new breed of enlightened men who could understand why these things had happened, and who would guide the people in the future. For many it was otherwise. In the Preface to *The Revolt of Islam* of 1818, Shelley tells how the panic at the excesses of the Revolution is gradually giving place to sanity, and declares his awareness of 'a slow, gradual, silent change'. Just before this he has spoken of how 'many of the most ardent and tender-hearted of the worshippers of public good have been morally ruined' by the destruction of their hopes, by what he describes as 'a partial glimpse of the events they deplored'. Partial it may well have been, though beside the breadth of Shelley's vision many understandings seem partial. But the effects of such moral ruin were felt for a long time.

Of the advances in scientific knowledge in Tennyson's age, few were more important than those of the geologist Charles Lyell (1797–1875). The discovery that the earth was immeasurably older than the few thousand years generally thought to have elapsed since Creation, left man desolate before the vast reaches of time. It is not surprising that the Victorians were obsessed by time, whether as 'the secular abyss to come' of *In Memoriam* 76 (LXXVI), or such an image of time past as the 'Dark bulks that tumble half alive, / And lazy lengths on boundless shores' of 70 (LXX). (The evolutionary sections of *In Memoriam*, such as 70, or the despairing 66 (LVI) ('"So careful of the type?" but no . . .'), were directly influenced by Lyell's *Principles of Geology*, which Tennyson read in 1837.) Probably the greatest shock to their sensibilities was Charles Darwin's (1809-1882) *On the Origin of Species* (1859), and the theory of Natural Selection which Darwin applied to man in *The Descent of Man* (1871). Lyell's conclusions about the mortality of species, and so of man, and the feeling that the indifference of nature might mean the indifference of God, were deeply troubling concepts. The reaction was no less troubling to many: opinion swung towards a soulless materialism which rejected purpose and design, the effects of which are only too much with us today. It was not possible for Tennyson to accommodate to his classic evolutionary beliefs, which meant an ultimate good appearing out of ill, and a crowning and godlike human race, the atomic and materialist beliefs of the age. Three years before his death, in 'Parnassus', he spoke of 'Astronomy and Geology, terrible Muses' towering with their 'deep double shadow' over the sacred fountain. Before this threat of space and time as interpreted by modern science, the reassurance of 'other songs for other worlds' seems weak. His insistence on individuality, and personal immortality, sometimes sounds like despair before the mental and physical abysses of the nineteenth-century universe.

Tennyson's work

Apart from the indifferent plays he composed late in life, Tennyson wrote only poetry. There are no treatises, and no fascinating records of thought, of the sort Coleridge left in his notebooks. He lived for poetry, although there is evidence that he doubted its authority. During his life he gained a large public in England and abroad, but long before he died some people were willing to believe that his day was over. Some critics, then and later, found a paradox in the spectacle of a man haunted by regret and loss who yet became the voice of the Victorian age. (It is, of course, much less of a paradox than it might appear.) In 1923 Harold Nicolson published an influential study, *Tennyson: Aspects of His Life, Character, and Poetry*, in which he argued that the public Tennyson flourished at the expense of the private man, who was the greater poet. The truth is more complex. Nevertheless the idea of the two Tennysons still lingers. His authority is in his extraordinary power over language, the subtleties of word and form by which he is heir to more than twenty centuries of European poetry. Anyone who thinks that this shows only a minor talent for language should reconsider the function of language. Critics of the second half of the twentieth century have often stressed his use of tradition, and his modernity. He is sometimes called either a Symbolist, or a precursor of the French Symbolist poets, such as Charles Baudelaire (1821–67) and Stéphane Mallarmé (1842–98). Ideally the Symbolist poem becomes a separate world or system, both the product and the instrument of vision. But although Tennyson's early poem 'Mariana', in which the woman's desolate state is objectified in a desolate house and landscape, may resemble Symbolism, it is hardly a closed system, in that we know exactly what is happening, and why. Neither is the late poem 'The Voice and the Peak' Symbolist, however it exalts the symbol itself.

Tennyson's greatest successes are in the idyll, the lyric, the monologue, and the short epistolary poem. His achievement in the longer poem is variable. *The Princess* of 1847 is a delightful but unequal narrative comedy, in the form of the mouth-to-mouth tale, by which a fantastic story is passed from narrator to narrator. The language has great charm, but the action strays into melodrama towards the end. *In Memoriam*, with *Maud* his major long work, is a single poem only by courtesy: a sequence of one hundred and thirty-three lyric elegies, of different length but in the same *abba* quatrain, in which a great grief is examined, and understood. The action is that of an exploration of possibilities, a continual movement of supposition, until faith in God's purposes is reaffirmed. *Maud* was a new form: a monodrama, in which the single speaker moves through twenty-six scenes of despair and loathing of a corrupt commercial society, of love, the death of the beloved, madness, and the strangely vulgar conclusion in which he recovers his sanity by going to fight, and probably to die, in the Crimea. It is a bold experiment, a representation of that distorted single vision of reality which we often regard as characteristic of modern art. In the *Idylls of the King*, composed at intervals over a period of forty years, he makes an extended use of the idyll form of which he was a master – comparable with the use Browning made of the monologue in *The Ring and the Book* – and with great skill depicts the ruin of man's kingdom, in the decline and fall of King Arthur's Camelot. Such loss is perhaps nearer to his heart than the triumph of the spirit in *In Memoriam*. But in considering the full effect of the *Idylls*, we have to take into account the frequent weaknesses of the archaising language, and its occasional air of earnest translation.

The problem of the nature and purpose of the long poem had haunted other poets besides Tennyson. Wordsworth struggled for years with the idea of a long poem, and the inferiority of *The Excursion* to the earlier poem *The Prelude* is a measure of his difficulties. Tennyson's long attachment to the Arthurian story (which Wordsworth, as well as Milton, had at one time considered as a subject), and the mingling of hesitation with a determination to make something of it, is roughly comparable. Nor is he among the most intellectual of poets. In reading Shelley we are always aware of Shelley's thinking about the mystery of being. In reading Tennyson, we are aware rather of his characteristic fears of meaninglessness. If the human will is often strong in him, the sense of darkness is even stronger. The tension between them is the source of some of his greatest effects. But the broadest and greatest effects, which we naturally and rightly associate with the long poem, are only intermittently present.

A note on the text

Tennyson's poems were published in various volumes between 1827 and 1892. The standard modern edition is that by Christopher Ricks, *The Poems of Tennyson*, Longman's Annotated English Poets, Longman, London, 1969, which omits the plays. Many of the poems discussed in these notes are in the selection (in the New Oxford English Series) from Tennyson's poems edited by Michael Millgate, Oxford University Press, Oxford, 1963. 'Frater Ave atque Vale' appears in the selection edited by Edmund Blunden, Heinemann Educational, London, 1968, and 'To E. Fitzgerald' in that edited by David Cecil, Faber and Faber, London, 1971. A useful selection is that made by John D. Jump, *'In Memoriam'*, *'Maud'* and *Other Poems*, Dent, London, 1975.

Part 2

Summaries
of SELECTED POEMS

THE POEMS ARE SUMMARISED in approximate chronological order. The text used for 'The Lady of Shalott' and 'The Lotos-Eaters' is that of 1842; both poems appeared in 1832, but were extensively revised for republication in 1842.

'Mariana' (1830)

Mariana was originally a character in Shakespeare's *Measure for Measure*, who had been cruelly deserted by her lover Angelo. The epigraph is founded on Shakespeare's 'There, at the moated grange, resides this dejected Mariana'. The poem is a series of pictures of the grange, the woman, and the country round the grange, making up a powerful evocation of the sadness of the house and of the woman who lives in it. The slight variations in the refrain serve to emphasise the weary monotony, whose force is felt in the marked variation in the last line: 'Oh God, that I were dead!' In the first stanza we approach the grange as observers, noting the details of its desolate state. What is most important, perhaps, is the mingling of mood and object. The device of the formal refrain is as old as poetry, but the prolonged objectification in house and landscape of the woman's desolation was a new note in English poetry.

NOTES AND GLOSSARY:
knots:	fastenings
Weeded:	having weeds growing on it
grange:	large country house, or manor

She said, 'I am aweary, aweary': l.11, like l.9, has an unstressed ending ('ăwearў̆'); the voice seems to sob. Note also the metrical variation in l.11, which has the same effect: the verse is iambic ($\cup$ /), but there is an extra syllable in 'ăwéarў̆, ắwéarў̆'

trance:	throw into a trance
casement:	window
athwart:	across
flats:	plains
night-fowl:	literally 'night-bird' or 'night-birds,' but 'crow' suggests a cock

fen:	marsh, with low fields
stone-cast:	stone's throw
sluice:	channel for draining water
marish:	marsh
leagues:	a league was usually about three miles
rounding gray:	gray (of sky or distance) which bounds the dreary landscape
up and away:	loosed, freed to go
their cell:	the cave of Aeolus, where in classical mythology the winds were bound
wainscot:	wooden panelling on lower part of interior walls
thick-moted:	motes are specks of dust

'The Lady of Shalott'   (1832, extensively revised for 1842)

Like 'Mariana', this poem is strongly pictorial. It is a symbolic tale of a lady condemned by a mysterious curse to weave ceaselessly a magic tapestry. The poem itself has something of the effect of a tapestry, notably in the description of the passers-by in Part II, but it is far from being a piece of sentimental medievalising. Part I shows us the island castle of Shalott, inhabited by the mysterious lady, and the road to Camelot, image of the external world of action. In Part II we move to the lady herself, weaving compulsively under the strange curse, seeing external reality only through the mirror she uses for her weaving, and seeing it as a pageant in which she has no part. In Part III, which takes place in harvest time, the magnificent Sir Lancelot, lover of Queen Guinevere, appears, riding to Camelot, and singing as he goes. The lady leaves her tapestry and looks down to Camelot, and the curse is fulfilled. In Part IV (autumn), the dying lady floats down the river to Camelot, singing her last song.

The stanzas continually contrast the active and external Camelot with the contemplative and withdrawn Shalott, except in Part III, where 'Lancelot' replaces 'Camelot' in stanza nine, and 'Shalott' in twelve. The four parts alternate between the external world, and the world of the lady. There is also a division between the contemplative present tenses of I and II, and the active past tenses of III and IV, prefigured by the first preterites in the poem in the last stanza of II: 'went', 'came', 'said'.

NOTES AND GLOSSARY:

wold:	open rolling country, often upland
Camelot:	the palace of King Arthur. The *Idylls of the King* tell of the fall of Camelot from its noble state into dissension, and crime. Here it merely represents the external world

Willows whiten, aspens quiver: These trees often grow beside water. The white underside of willow leaves shows when the wind blows them; aspens quiver at the least breath of wind

dusk: darken; the water darkens under the breeze

imbowers: embowers, encloses; shelters

shallop: skiff or light craft

bearded barley: barley ears have long bristles

cheerly: cheeringly

web: cloth, here tapestry

churls: men of low degree, or louts

damsels: girls (*French* demoiselles)

pad: quiet easy-paced horse

greaves: leg armour

A red-cross knight: Lancelot's knightly emblem, or arms

blazoned baldric: shoulder strap for the bugle, with his arms blazoned on it

'Tirra lirra': as in Autolycus's song in Shakespeare's *The Winter's Tale*, IV.2.9

is come: has come

waning: losing strength or size

seër: prophet or visionary

mischance: misfortune

tide: moving water

burgher: rich citizen of a burgh or town

what is here?: what is happening?

cheer: feasting, revelry

'St Simeon Stylites' (1842)

This superb dramatic monologue was written in 1833, when Tennyson was twenty-three or twenty-four. Its satiric force and savage humour, although characteristic of the man, only rarely appear in his poetry. (For a comparison, see the juvenile dramatic fragment 'The Devil and the Lady'; some parts of *The Princess*; *Maud*; 'Locksley Hall'; and the two Northern Farmer poems.) The dramatic monologue is a nineteenth- and twentieth-century mode in which the speaker tells us something about himself, and often unconsciously tells us more about himself than he realises, as here. 'The Love Song of J. Alfred Prufrock' of T.S. Eliot (1888–1965) is a modern example. Tennyson's contemporary Robert Browning (1812–89) is generally considered to be the great master of the form, although 'St Simeon Stylites' was written a little before any of Browning's monologues. 'Ulysses' and 'Tithonus' (then 'Tithon') were written in the same year. 'Demeter and Persephone'

(1889) is a fine late example. St Simeon spent many years on a column in Syria, mortifying himself to obtain a closer knowledge of God. Tennyson had little sympathy with asceticism of this sort, and presents Simeon as a neurotic and indeed half crazy hypocrite, whose one desire is to be made a saint.

(1–20) Although (he says) he is the basest of mankind, Simeon still hopes to be a saint, and will not cease to assault heaven with prayers. He prays for forgiveness, but in reality he does not think of himself as base. In support of his claim, he reminds God that he has spent thirty years on his pillar (*stulos* is the Greek for pillar), in spite of illness and bad weather, and speaks of his disappointment at not yet having been received into sainthood. (21–44) Not (he says) that he complains: the weight of sin was much worse than these pains. When young he was better able to bear them; now feeble, he hopes for death, and though half deaf, almost blind, and rotting, he will continue to cry to God. (45–58) Surely he deserves sainthood. Other holy martyrs died once, but his sufferings have been a life of death. If he could have suffered more, he would have done so. (59–118) He lists his other sufferings, in the convent, where the rope of penance gave him an ulcer; on the mountain, naked to the elements, chained to the rock, where he worked miracles, and cured the sick; three years crouched on a pillar, three years on a higher pillar, and twenty years on this one, the highest. His mind is confused, but he thinks this is an accurate record. Yet sometimes evil spirits perplex him. Nevertheless God should remember that while He and the saints are in heaven, and men live happily on earth, Simeon, weak and wretched, performs his ceaseless devotions. Again (as in lines 8, 44, 83, 118) he prays for forgiveness. (119–30) Sinful as he is, God will understand he is not to blame if the foolish people worship him. 'I am nothing – they think I am a saint – and indeed I have suffered more than many saints'. (131–42) The people round the column ought not to kneel to him, a sinner. Perhaps he has performed some miracles, and suffered more than any saint; it hardly matters. But they may remain kneeling. If any of them is crippled, he can heal him. [Presumably at this point someone accepts his offer, and something resembling an act of healing takes place.] (143–94) Simeon triumphs in his supposed power. Since he works miracles, he must be a saint, hearing the crowd's voice, and other mysterious voices, which may be produced by his diseased state. His hope is now strong, that God has forgiven his sins. He addresses the people again on the subject of his sins, paid for by a long penance by which surely he has also bought sanctity. He describes how devils tormented him, and could be subdued only by penance. This is the path the people must follow. But God is to be praised, not Simeon, God who has made Simeon an outstanding example. Yet perhaps now – even now – they may worship him, now that he is surely a saint. (195–220) Even as he speaks, pain afflicts him, and his eyes darken. A shadow, a light? The angel with the crown! He clutches, loses, and clutches it again, the sweet-smelling crown: surely this is the moment of his great translation. He asks for a priest to climb up to him, and give him the last sacrament before his death, and prays that the people may follow his example.

NOTES AND GLOSSARY:

Stylites:	of the pillar (*Greek* 'stulos')
slough:	outer skin which drops off
meet:	fit
avail:	be of use
thrice:	three times. The number is formulaic, or traditional
stitches:	pains, usually in the side
throes:	convulsions
meed:	what is due to, or deserved by
palm:	the palm branch was a symbol of victory or merit
hale:	healthy, strong
tagged:	fringed
hum:	make a low murmuring sound, such as a crowd of people makes
piecemeal:	by pieces, fragments
Who may be saved?:	see the Bible, Matthew 19: 25: 'When his disciples heard it, they were exceedingly amazed, saying, Who then can be saved?'
stinted practice:	spared action
haled:	drew
marvelled:	wondered
whereof:	of which
Pent:	confined
close:	narrow space
Inswathed:	rolled in (the image is of wrappings)
damps:	wet places
palsies:	paralyses
cover:	see the Bible, Psalm 85: 2
cubits:	the cubit was a measure of about eighteen inches, or from the elbow to the tip of the middle finger
slow light:	the sun
dial:	the metaphor is of a sundial, or sunclock, usually on a column
prate:	talk foolishly
crackling:	the sound made by a stiffened fabric; here, in his diseased fancy, by hard frost
undressed:	untanned

strive and wrestle: see the Bible, Genesis 32: 24
wash away my sins: see the Bible, Acts 22: 16
conceived and born in sin: see the Bible, Psalm 51: 5

Lay it not to me:	do not accuse me of it
calendared:	registered in the calendar of saints
halt:	lame (people)
hark:	hearken, listen
not told:	that is, in the holy records, principally the Bible
saint me:	call me saint, hail me as a saint
ere:	before
archives:	collections of records
hoar with rime:	white with frost

my high nest of penance: this is a most revealing paradox

Pontius, Iscariot:	Pontius Pilate, the Roman Governor of Judaea who condemned Christ, and Judas Iscariot, the disciple who betrayed him
seraphs:	highest orders of angels
vessel:	pot, receptacle
Abaddon:	the angel of the bottomless pit
Asmodeus:	Prince of the demons
hoggish:	pig-like
this way:	that is, mortifying his flesh
scourges:	whips. 'Thorns' in this context is reminiscent of the crowning of Christ with thorns, after scourging
Smite:	strike
spare:	refrain from punishing or harming
Lent:	period of fasting before the Christian festival of Easter

I do not say / But that: the effect is that of a dishonestly cautious affirmation

relics:	literally, the things I shall leave behind. Relics of saints are valued
gathered to:	joined with, becoming one of; most frequently of death, as in 'gathered to his fathers'
shrewdest:	keenest
draw nigh:	come near
the crown:	suggesting the crown of life in the Bible, Revelation 2: 10

spikenard, balm, frankincense: precious aromatic ointments

shaft:	column
the blessed sacrament:	the body and blood of Christ, in the form of consecrated bread and wine. Simeon asks for the last sacrament, given before death

'The Lotos-Eaters'	(1832, extensively revised for 1842)

The main source is Homer's *Odyssey*, book 9, 82–104. There are two parts: the five narrative Spenserian stanzas, and the irregular Choric Song of the mariners who eat the lotos fruit, which drugs them into a passive dreamlike state. (The Spenserian stanza was invented by the sixteenth-century poet Edmund Spenser, and used in his unfinished *The Faerie Queene*. The stanza is of nine lines, rhyming *ababbcbcc*; the last line is an Alexandrine, of six iambic feet.) No poem of Tennyson's is more melodious. The question is often asked, how far he approved of the passive state. He may have been able to indulge his fascination with passivity, knowing that in Homer Odysseus (or Ulysses) forced his drugged mariners back to the ship. But the return is not described in his poem.

Ulysses encourages his weary mariners. They find a strange land, where life moves slowly; even the stream falling from the cliff seems slow. With its waters and shady places, the land seems to welcome them. The sunset seems enchanted, lingering as if unwilling to end; inland are valleys, vales, and meadows; a strange land, 'where all things always seemed the same'. The Lotos-Eaters, or natives of this land, offer the mariners the lotos fruit. Tasting it, they drop out of life into a waking dream, in which the everyday sounds of the sea, and of their companions' voices, are distant and strange. Sitting on the shore, they dream of home, but think with loathing of the sea and the heavy oar, and sing, as if with one voice, 'We will no longer roam'.

The choric songs of the drugged sailors alternates between the delicious present, and their hateful past of war and the devouring sea. (Ulysses and his men are on their way home to the Greek island of Ithaca, after the ten years' war at Troy.) In I they sing of the strange music of lotos-land, which is in their minds and blood. In II they reason on the human condition, advancing the classic paradox of man as the highest being, who lives in torment, and the classic claim that calm is the crown of life. III presents the analogy of growing things happy in their natural cycle: the leaf, the apple which 'hath no toil'. IV returns to the human condition: they no longer question, but reject, in brief sullen sentences, asking at the end for death, or 'dreamful ease'. V is the projected dream, now become reality, of peace in lotos-land: a life of lulled and sweetened senses, and whispered speech, of grateful distant memories of childhood, and the dead. VI follows these memories with a rationalisation of present, and past: surely their families have forgotten them, and Ithaca has been seized. There is nothing they can do about it; 'there *is* confusion worse than death', to men who have endured so much. But (VII) the wonderful dewy freshness of lotos-land, its many prospects, and luxuriance! The lotos (VIII) grows everywhere, and will sustain them. No more of the toil and peril of the seas; they will live here like Gods, the Gods who lead their own lives, careless of the suffering of mankind.

NOTES AND GLOSSARY:

he: Ulysses, King of Ithaca

land ... land (ll.1 and 3): a no-rhyme, said by Tennyson to be more lazy than the first reading of 'land ... strand.'

did swoon: 'swoon' means 'faint'. The construction is periphrastic (using more words than necessary), and archaic. There are several of these periphrases in the first five stanzas, all giving the effect of a slow wondering observation

a weary dream: a nightmare

lawn: finely woven linen

Rolling ... below: that is, rolling below a slumbrous sheet of foam

Upclomb: climbed up (archaic)

down: grassy open highland or upland, sometimes called downland

galingale: plant or tree with aromatic roots

keel: that is, ship. Unless (as is likely) the ship is beached, when it literally means the keel of the ship

rave: (literally) talk wildly

blown: full-bloomed

tired ... tired: Tennyson indicated the length of the word as 'tïërd', but added 'making the word neither monosyllabic nor dissyllabic, but a dreamy child of the two'

make ... moan: lament

steep: bathe, soak

waxing: growing or increasing

Fast-rooted: firmly rooted

Vaulted: arched like a roof

parcels: pieces

myrrh: aromatic plant

crisping: curling

urn: that is, urn in which the ashes of the dead were placed

Our sons inherit us: a recurrent theme in Tennyson: see section 90 (XC) of *In Memoriam*, and 'Enoch Arden'

the little isle: that is, Ithaca

amaranth: legendary unfading flower

moly: fabulous herb with magic properties

lowly:	softly (unusual as an adverb in this sense)
acanthus:	plant, whose leaf form was much used in Greek architecture as an ornamental pattern
blows:	blooms
starboard, larboard:	right and left side of vessel looking forward
with an equal mind:	calmly and firmly
nectar:	the drink of the gods
bolts:	thunderbolts, or lightning flashes, the weapons of the gods
Blight:	malignant influence
cleave:	cut (that is, plough)
Elysian:	Elysium was the abode of the blessed after death
asphodel:	immortal flower in Elysium

'Ulysses' (1842)

This dramatic monologue was written in October 1833, soon after Tennyson heard of Hallam's death. He said of it: 'it gives the feeling about the need of going forward and braving the struggle of life perhaps more simply than anything in *In Memoriam*'. Ulysses, or Odysseus, who appears briefly in 'The Lotos-Eaters', was one of the Greek kings who besieged and took Troy; his long wanderings and homecoming are told in the *Odyssey* of Homer. Another last voyage for Ulysses occurs in *The Divine Comedy* of Dante (1265–1321), (*Inferno*, 26, 90ff.). Tennyson makes him an old man bored with his island kingdom, and desiring one more voyage of adventure before death. The first and third of the four paragraphs are short, the second and fourth long. In the fourth paragraph he addresses his old companions. It is generally supposed that paragraph three is also spoken aloud, although it gains something if regarded as internal monologue. 'Ulysses' is capable of several interpretations; there has been a long critical debate about whether he is heroic, or less than heroic, in leaving his subjects and his aged wife.

(1–5) Ulysses speaks of his inaction on Ithaca, with his wife Penelope, among his brutish subjects. (6–32) He speaks of his love of life, of his great name, of all that he has seen and known, and of how there is always something more to be experienced. Life must be used; it would be unmanly to spare himself in old age, while longing to follow knowledge beyond its human limits. (33–43) His son Telemachus will take his place, and will instruct and civilise the Ithacans. Unlike Ulysses, his talents are civil, and domestic: 'He works his work, I mine'. (44–70) The ship is ready. Ulysses turns to his old companions who will accompany him, and recalls what they have known together. Old though they are, they may yet accomplish one more heroic deed. The deep seas call them; they will sail west into unknown waters, perhaps to see the great hero Achilles, 'whom we knew'. They are not the men they were, but accept their fate, knowing that their hearts are great.

NOTES AND GLOSSARY:

still hearth: in part an image of a dead fire, but also that of a house without children

an agèd wife: Penelope, who had remained faithful during his long absence. It is his only mention of her

mete and dole: measure out carefully: 'dole' suggests small quantities, and the phrase strongly suggests day-to-day dullness

Unequal laws: laws made for a primitive race, in that their weight varies among different classes of society

lees: the dregs of wine

scudding drifts: to scud is to move quickly; drifts are broken clouds

Hyades: stars whose rising predicted storm

ringing: probably ringing with the sounds of battle

I am a part of all that I have met: a subtle variation on the more usual 'all that I have met is a part of me'

arch: this image has been much discussed; it probably suggests a rainbow

Gleams: a word of particular meaning in Tennyson, suggesting a light which is to be followed; see the late poem 'Merlin and the Gleam'

of me: (*archaic*) by me

discerning to: clear-sighted enough to be able to

rugged: rough, strong. Notice that 'the savage race' of l.4 is now only 'a rugged people', as Ulysses leaves the Ithacans to his son

blameless: a high attribute in a heroic age, and indeed in any age in which men know that evil exists

sphere: path (the sphere of a planet was its appointed track in the heavens)

decent: knowing what is fitting (compare the structure of 'discerning to fulfil' in l.35)

household gods: gods of the hearth and home

wrought: worked. Note the rhyme of 'thought,' which follows 'wrought' with the suddenness of a new understanding of what he had in common with his companions; the difference from his attitude to Telemachus is marked, although there is no contempt towards him

frolic: playful

Not unbecoming: the understatement of the double negative is

	appropriate to such persuasion
sitting well in order:	that is, at the oars. Vessels of the heroic age were rowed by the warriors, sometimes with the king as helmsman; the galleys of a later age were rowed by slaves
gulfs:	the deeps of the sea, or perhaps the abysses believed to lie beyond the ocean that circled the world
wash:	(of a moving liquid) carry along. This line is entirely monosyllabic, like several others in the last sentence
touch:	idiomatic: for example, 'the ship touched at several ports'. Tennyson brilliantly combines this with a sense of the hesitation before the impossible
the Happy Isles:	the Isles of the Blessed, believed to lie in the western ocean
abides:	remains
To strive . . . not to yield:	that this line has the same cadence as the fifth line is probably significant

---

'Break, break, break' (1842)

This short lyric was probably written in 1834. It was inspired by the death of Hallam. No summary is necessary, or indeed possible, although it should be noted that the eye moves from the breaking waves to the children on the shore, then from the young sailor in his boat on the bay to the ships farther out, then back to the sea breaking on the stones. The movement is circular, and the poem ends with the despair and inability to understand with which it began. The rhythm is anapaestic: ◡ ◡ ╱. Anapaests are usually associated with lightness and speed; Tennyson's anapaests here are very slow. Apart from the remorseless and hopeless breaking of the sea on the rocks, the poem seems content with observation in place of imagery. This is probably its essential meaning: the world is meaningless.

NOTES AND GLOSSARY:

O well for:	in a double sense: that is, it is well for him, but not for me; and also it is well for him, since he does not know what the future will bring. The phrase is ironic
stately:	the power of this adjective in its context is that the ships, though stately and dignified, are vulnerable. Wordsworth has a comparable effect in his sonnet 'Composed upon Westminster Bridge', where he speaks of the great sleeping city as a sight 'touching in its majesty'
haven:	harbour

'Come down, O maid, from yonder mountain height'
(from *The Princess* (1847))

This is one of the two lyrics from the last section of *The Princess*. In this section Princess Ida, who has rejected men because of their assumption of superiority over women, finally accepts the love of the Prince. The Prince's belief is that man must gain in sweetness, woman in 'mental breadth,' until at last woman will 'set herself to man, / Like perfect music unto noble words'. The other song in this section is 'Now sleeps the crimson petal, now the white,' which is a variation on the Persian *ghazal* form. The lyrics within the verse of *The Princess* – 'Tears, idle tears', 'O Swallow, Swallow', 'Our enemies have fallen', and the two already referred to – should not be confused with the six intercalary (inserted) songs between the seven sections, which Tennyson added in 1850. Ida reads this song or 'small sweet idyl' as she sits by the bed of the Prince, who has persisted in his wooing of her, and is now recovering from wounds received at a tounament between his supporters and Ida's. The lyric is a classic example of the seduction song, like 'To His Coy Mistress' by Andrew Marvell (1621–78). The shepherd, who is a type or figure of the pastoral lover, begs the virgin to leave the cold and sterile heights of virginity, where nothing that is human can be found. He asks her to come down to the warm human valley, where Love lives with contentment, and to follow the falling stream to the hearth and home that await her. On the icy mountains the only sound is the yelping of the savage eagles, but in the valley every sound is sweet. The poem ends with three lines of extraordinary onomatopoeia invoking the characteristic sounds of the sheltered valley. This rich onomatopoeia, or imitation of sound, is an appropriate conclusion: the virgin is being called back to that richness of life which she seems to have abandoned. Notice that from the beginning the shepherd assumes, perhaps as a stratagem, that she is looking for love.

NOTES AND GLOSSARY:

glide a sunbeam: that is, like a sunbeam

the blasted Pine: withered, blighted pine tree. The pine is common in northern latitudes, and is able to grow at great heights. Here its state symbolises the sterility of the mountains

spire: tapering structure, or tower: here 'peak'

threshold: symbolising the house, with its frequent comings and goings

spirted purple of the vats: grape juice splashing as it is trodden

foxlike in the vine: the reference is to the Bible, Song of Solomon 2: 15: 'Take us the foxes, the little foxes that spoil the

	vines; for our vines have tender grapes'
silver horns:	the white snowy peaks, here made emblematic. There is probably a reference to the crescent moon of Diana, goddess of virginity, hunting, and the moon
firths:	that is, glaciers; usually arms of the sea, or estuaries, as in *In Memoriam*, Epilogue, l.116 (see below)
furrow-cloven:	split by deep wrinkles, or hollows
to roll the torrent:	that is, the cold streams from the ice
dance thee down:	the virgin is to follow the dancing waters on their way down to make the valley fruitful
water-smoke:	see 'The Lotos-Eaters', l.10
like a broken purpose:	the simile refers directly to the waste of nature's purposes in virginity. It is an old argument

---

From *In Memoriam* (1850)

For convenience, the usual Roman numbering is indicated in brackets.

Section 7 (vii)
One of the very late additions to *In Memoriam*, just before publication. It returns to the great grief, although since it occurs early in the sequence it in no sense counters the optimism of the sequence. The hand is that of Hallam. Tennyson, after a sleepless night in London, goes before dawn to his dead friend's house, where he has so often been a welcome guest. The house is silent, his friend is dead; elsewhere life begins again with the new day, and its blank cold light.

NOTES AND GLOSSARY:

dark house:	67 Wimpole Street, London. There may be a suggestion of the classic image of the dead body as a deserted house, here reversed
a hand:	the image of the hand recurs in the sequence, as in 10 (x), l.19, and 55 (lv), l.17.
Behold me:	the tone of this is bitter
like a guilty thing:	as with the ghost in Shakespeare's *Hamlet* I.1.148: 'And then it started like a guilty thing'. See also Wordsworth's 'Ode: Intimations of Immortality', ll.150−1: 'High instincts before which our mortal Nature / Did tremble like a guilty Thing surprised'
He is not here:	see the Bible, as in Luke 24:6, where the angels at the empty tomb say of Christ, 'He is not here, but is risen'
noise of life:	the suggestion ('noise') is of something disordered, lacking harmony

On the bald street breaks the blank day: note the strong alliteration of 'bald . . . breaks . . . blank'; above all, the virtual abandoning of the iambic verse (◡ / ◡ / ◡ / ◡ /) in 'On thĕ báld stréet breăks thĕ blánk day'.

bald: because empty of traffic at this early hour. (Traffic is beginning to move in the busier Oxford Street.) The camber or slight curve in the street is also noticeable when it is empty, which may have helped Tennyson to this image

blank: empty, meaningless. Compare 'Break, break, break'

Section 34 (xxxiv)

With 35, this forms an argument the to-and-from movement of which suggests a dialogue; the effect is frequent in *In Memoriam*, which is above all a hesitant and very human progress from despair and doubt to hope and faith. Note that after the first stanza the argument passes almost insensibly – marked by the subjunctive 'were' of l.9 – to a saddened acceptance of materialism and mortality. I should have learned that life is immortal; that if it is not, nothing lives, this world and sun being meaningless, like the work of a heedless artist, and its God unknowable; surely it would be best to die.

NOTES AND GLOSSARY:

conscience: understanding, with perhaps a suggestion of moral conscience

such as I: that is, to those who do not believe in immortality

charming: the snake was supposed to draw its prey to it by the hypnotic power of its eye, and the fear which it inspired

cease: see Keats's 'To cease upon the midnight with no pain' ('Ode to a Nightingale'). What Keats plays with as a pleasing thought horrifies Tennyson

Section 35 (xxxv)

The debate of 34 is continued. The turns of the argument sometimes work against the verse structure, as in l.5, where a thought is countered almost before it has time to form.

Yet if a true voice spoke from the grave of final death, might I not say, 'Love, I strive to keep alive hope of eternal life'? But I should hear desolate time at its work of levelling and building, and Love would answer, 'The very thought of vast time would enfeeble me'. Yet why argue foolishly? If death were accepted as final, there would have been no love, or what love there was would have been merely sensual and vicious.

Section 35, and with it the single unit of 34 and 35, seems to end with love's triumph. But the last stanza betrays its fascination with mortality in the lingering over love's coarsest satyr-shape.

NOTES AND GLOSSARY:

the narrow house: the grave

The cheeks . . . in dust: With 'Yet,' after the conclusion of 34, one expects the voice from the grave to offer hope, but it does not

even here: that is, on this imperfect earth

O Love: the first inspiration of the sequence, and its most powerful principle

homeless: a word of great power; compare Wordsworth's 'the homeless voice of waters' (*The Prelude*, XIV), and Shelley, 'The thunder and the hiss of homeless streams' ('Alastor')

Aeonian: aeon, or eon, means an immeasurable period

to be: which will be

forgetful: bringing forgetfulness

case: sum of arguments, or argument

as Death: sum of arguments, or argument

in narrowest working shut: confined to a very narrow function

Satyr: legendary creature, half-man, half-goat (the shape of the god Pan), and a type of brutish sensuality: see 'Lucretius', ll.192–9. There as here Tennyson expresses his disgust for sensual love

battened: (would have) fed gluttonously

basked and battened: 'bask' suggests something passive, 'batten' is an action hardly better than passive

Section 49 (XLIX)

A moment of near despair, despite the ocasional comfort he has found. With 50 (L), it is one of the darkest of the elegies. The principal image is that of a lake whose sullen surface is broken up and varied by a number of influences, but whose depths remain dark. The first three stanzas deal with the surface, the fourth with the unchanging depths.

NOTES AND GLOSSARY:

the schools: the universities, with their various schools or faculties of theology and philosophy

glance: there are several meanings: a look, or a flash of light, or a blow which glides or glances off an object instead of striking it full

lisp: speak softly and with a child's intonation

wreathe: that is, move in the shape of a wreath or circle (see 'eddy')

look thy look: addressed, with a slight suggestion of derogation, to a passer-by, who cannot be expected to understand

tender-pencilled: delicately drawn, or painted

fancied hopes and fears: note that the real sorrow is deeper even than fancied fears

muffled motions: obscure hidden movements

bases: the image may be of the land or hills about the lake; see 'Morte d'Arthur', l.274

Section 56 (LVI)

A late addition to the sequence. The argument of 54 and 55 ends with 'I...faintly trust the larger hope', having spoken of strife between God and Nature, and of Nature as 'careless of the single life', though 'careful of the type', or species. Section 56 denies this last, quoting from 55, and returning on its clouded affirmation with the fear that even man will pass away. The nineteenth-century debate between man as divinely inspired, and the nature of modern scientific and materialist theory, has never been more brilliantly expressed. The 'scarpèd cliff and quarried stone' of the first stanza refer to the geological evidence of the death of species.

NOTES AND GLOSSARY:

scarpèd: steeply sloped, especially by erosion or faulting; here exposing the strata

types: species. Tennyson often uses 'type' to mean an example or characteristic specimen, as in the last stanza but one of the Epilogue

rolled: loudly uttered

fanes: temples

Nature, red in tooth and claw: that is, the Nature of a pitiless struggle for survival

ravine: seizing and devouring of prey; compare 'raven'

Be blown: the construction of the sentence is 'shall he' (l.8) 'be blown'

the prime: the first age

tare: tear

thy voice: that is, Hallam's voice

redress: remedy, for injustice

Behind the veil: there is probably no precise origin for this; the veil which will not be drawn in this life is a common image

Section 88 (LXXXVIII)

This is the third of three successive elegies in which the mourner is thinking now of life rather than death: the peace of 86, the delight in what has been of 87, and now in 88 the nightingale as the voice of life. The song of the nightingale is a classic image of passion, sorrow, and joy. Tennyson finds in it the extremes which war within himself, and in the third stanza recognises that however possessed by sorrow he seems to be, the glory of the richness of life is not to be denied.

NOTES AND GLOSSARY:

Wild bird: the nightingale is 'wild' because of the power and passion of its song

Rings Eden: 'rings' expresses the echoing power of the song; Tennyson glossed 'Eden' as 'a paradisal song'

quicks: quickset thorns or hedge-rows

employ: occupy, keep occupied

darkening: that is, as night comes on

harp: the harp is often synonymous with a poet's song, like the lyre

all command the strings: command all the strings, or entirely command the strings

the sum of things: all things; 'sum' suggests also a momentary flash of understanding: see 'go'

Will flash: that is, will flash whether or not I want it to

Section 95 (xcv)
The climax of a series of elegies, in which the possibility has grown of direct contact with Hallam's spirit. The contact here is by means of 'the noble letters of the dead,' and is strictly factual. What Tennyson experiences, after the trance into which he falls, is once again a sense of fuller life.

The sixteen stanzas are divided into four groups of four. In the first group, the large family of brothers and sisters are on the lawn at Somersby Rectory on a calm summer night round the tea-urn, singing old or traditional songs. In the second Tennyson, lingering alone after the others have retired, reads Hallam's letters again, thinking how strange it is to hear his voice in them. The third presents the trance into which he falls, which is probably brought on by strong desire for spiritual contact, together with Hallam's ambiguous presence in the letters. In this trance he seems to find 'that which is', and to hear what might be the music of eternity. In the fourth part he is returned to the present scene, animated now by a breeze, precursor of the dawn, and symbol of life.

NOTES AND GLOSSARY:

And genial warmth...drawn: the grammatical connection between ll.3−6 and 1−2 is slight. See the note on 121, l.4

tapers: candles

cricket:	a jumping chirping insect
chirred:	onomatopoeic, indicating the prolonged trilling sound characteristic of crickets and grasshoppers
fluttering urn:	referring to the sound of the small flame under the tea-urn
lit:	alit (from 'alight'), settled
filmy:	gauzy (Tennyson may also be thinking of the hazy effect of rapidly beating wings)
shapes . . . dusk:	that is, the night-moths. The construction is 'the (moths) wheeled or lit'
ermine:	white and furry
knoll:	small hill, mound
couched:	lying
kine:	cattle
the trees . . . field:	the first of the four sections or groups ends with an image of the trees as human, which is the climax of the unthreatening nature so intimately shown
from me and night:	see Thomas Gray's (1716−71) 'Elegy in a Country Churchyard', 1.4: 'And leaves the world to darkness and to me'
that glad year:	the friendship lasted for over four years. The reference to a single year may be formulaic (that is, following a poetic convention)
leaves:	the image is of dead (yet living) leaves, but there is also the idea of leaf meaning 'page'
doubts:	see Section 96 (XCVI), ll.13−16, on Hallam's conquest of his religious doubts
inmost cell:	the image is biological
seemed:	'the dead man' in the preceding line is uncompromising, and since what follows is directed by 'seems', it cannot be taken for the contact he had dreamed of achieving. Many critics have overlooked this
The living soul:	the 1850−70 reading was 'His', with 'his' for 'this' in 1.37. Tennyson said he often had 'that feeling of being whirled up and rapt into the great Soul'. He was uneasy about the 1850−70 reading, perhaps for religious reasons, but it is nevertheless preferable
empyreal:	from 'empyrean', or the highest heaven and abode of God
came on:	found, as if by accident
that which is:	the reality of the Divine
frame:	express, cast

matter-moulded:	moulded by sensible experience, and so unfit to express further experience
doubtful:	ambiguous, uncertain. See note on 'East . . . lights' below
sucked:	this is passive, referring to 'the breeze'
East . . . lights:	in northern latitudes in June the last light of one day and the first light of the next can be very close to each other. The dusk in 1.49 is perhaps 'doubtful' also because it is hard to say to which day it belongs

Section 107 (CVII)

For the first time in the sequence, Hallam's birthday is celebrated. (Sections 72 (LXXII) and 99 (XCIX) speak of the anniversary of his death.) The affirmation in this is supported by the acceptance of death, and the strong will to live. There is no more thought of spiritual contact with the dead. The dead season can offer no flowers, the land is gripped by icy cold, and snow falls in the winter sea. But with wine and food, and fires against the cold, they will keep Hallam's birthday. There will be no sorrow, and no desolate yearning. The poem should be compared with 108 (CVIII), where Tennyson declares, 'I will not shut me from my kind' (that is, mankind), and admits how profitless it is to 'eat [his] heart alone'.

NOTES AND GLOSSARY:

the day:	1 February 1811; a short winter's day
bitter day:	the bitterness is that of the season, unlike the anniversary of his death
vapour:	cloud. 'Bank' means a flat-topped mass
leaving night forlorn:	this is obscure, but the sense seems to be that the short cold day brought in a desolate and hopeless night; again, the desolation is that of the season
time:	season
admits not:	permits not. Notice the laconic tone: there cannot be any flowers, and there is nothing more to be said about it
deck:	decorate
the blast of North and East:	the coldest winds in Europe
eaves:	overhanging edges of roofs, from which the icicles hang like knife blades
bristles . . . crescent:	the hard ice causes thickets (brakes) and thorns to stiffen at ('to') the crescent moon, like the bristles or rough hairs of an animal, which rise when its temper is roused
grides:	makes scrape together with grating sound

leafless ribs and iron horns: winter branches, made rigid by the icy cold; the image is that of a starving but defiant animal

drifts: fine snow driven by the wind

darken: according to Tennyson's son Hallam Tennyson, who must have heard it from his father, this refers to the darkening of the snow as it falls into the sea

breaks: breaks on (of waves), but also meaning the breaking down of land by sea

brim: fill to the brim (with wine)

even as he were by: just as if he were here with us

whate'er he be: whatever the dead Hallam is now, we will drink to him. The phrase contrasts strongly with the former longing for contact with his spirit

Section 121 (CXXI)

One of the last elegies written, which shows that not all the later sections were pessimistic, as is sometimes suggested. At the end of Section 95 East and West became one; this poem turns on the fact that Hesper the evening star, and Phosphor the morning star, are in fact the same star. The first two stanzas speak of the evening star and what it sees and hears on earth as darkness comes; the third and fourth stanzas are about the morning star, and the awakening world. In the final stanza the poet takes their identity as 'Hesper-Phosphor' as an image of his unchanging happy past, and present.

NOTES AND GLOSSARY.

dim / And dimmer: that is, progressively

and a glory done: the phrase is typical of Tennyson's occasionally (and deliberately) loose syntax in *In Memoriam*; see 95, ll.1−8

team: of horses

wain: wagon, usually a farm wagon

life . . . brain: that is, with sleep

the greater light: the sun. Compare the Bible, Genesis 1:16

the village hammer: that of the village blacksmith, who shoed the horses

clink: make a sharp ringing sound

Section 130 (CXXX)

Hallam is not lost to Tennyson; he is still loved, though seeming to be a power in nature. In spite of this, he is perhaps loved even more; he is distant, but near, not to be lost now in life or death.

NOTES AND GLOSSARY:

standest: see the Bible, Revelation 19:17

seem:	the use of this word in ll.6 and 12 means that there is no self-deceit; see 95, l.35. But notice 'feel thee some diffusive power', not 'feel thee as some diffusive power'
diffusive:	that is, a power which sends itself forth
circled:	there is a sense of 'protected' in the word

From the Epilogue (ll.101–44, i.e. the last eleven stanzas of *In Memoriam*)
So named not by Tennyson, but by the critics, who also named the Prologue; both titles have been generally accepted. The Epilogue celebrates the marriage of Tennyson's friend Edmund Lushington to his sister, Cecilia Tennyson. Hallam had been engaged to his sister Emily, and in the first part of the Epilogue Tennyson describes how, while the healths of Cecilia and Edmund Lushington are being drunk, he guesses at the presence of 'a stiller guest' perhaps among them. The first ninety lines or so of the Epilogue are generalised, and rather commonplace, as are a number of other domestic scenes and images in the sequence. (See, for example, 6 (VI), ll.25–40.) But the single sentence of the last forty-four lines shows Tennyson at the height of his powers. Characteristically, he retires from the festivities, and with that the poetry becomes visionary, as he turns from the everyday aspect of the marriage to what it represents. His imagination follows the bridal couple to where they spend the first night of their married life; to the mystery of the conception of their child, a soul made flesh, who will bring mankind even nearer to the great race that will be; the 'crowning race' from whom nothing will be hidden, the climax of the long human struggle towards perfection; that race of which the man he knew, who now lives in God, was an early and a noble type.

NOTES AND GLOSSARY:

glee:	mirth, or a song (a musical composition for three or more voices)
shade of passing thought:	possibly of Hallam (as in ll.85–8), but not necessarily: see l.93
the three-times-three:	three cheers three times repeated, as the appropriate climax to all the healths drunk to the newly married couple
that tower:	that is, the church spire with its bells, now silent. Speaking towers are frequently found in legend. Note the force of the inversion, at this moment of change of mood to the visionary
rising fire:	that of the moon, but 'fire' takes it back to a primitive feeling of a supernatural visitation
down and ... dale:	hills and valleys

white-faced halls:	moonlit fronts of large country houses
rills:	small streams, rivulets
friths:	firths; that is, arms of the sea, or, as here, estuaries
the splendour:	that is, of the moonlight
spangle:	a spangle is a small disc of glittering material, often sewn on dresses as ornament. Although it follows logically from 'breaking', Tennyson risks something in using it here
the happy shores:	the couple spent their wedding night by the sea
system:	as in 'solar system'
rolling:	the subject is 'a soul'
draw:	move
the vast:	the deep of space and time
strike ... bounds:	the reference is to the new soul embodied at conception, and confined within the bounds of flesh. 'Strike' suggests a sudden action; the suddenness reflects the mystery of creation
move ... phase:	the reference is to the theory that the human embryo reproduces the stages of the different forms of life
eye to eye:	directly
half-akin to brute:	'akin' means related, or of similar or kindred character. As often, Tennyson is troubled by what he thought of as the animal side of man; see the close of 35 (xxxv), and also of 118 (cxviii): 'Move upward, working out the beast, / And let the ape and tiger die'
is:	the present tenses in ll.131, 132, 135, and 136 are anticipatory
element:	that which is uncompounded or essential or irreducible; Latin *elementum* means a first principle

---

'The Golden Year' (1846)

This poem is in the tradition of 'English Idyls' such as 'Audley Court' and 'Walking to the Mail', of 1842, and was probably written at about the same time, in the late 1830s. Like these poems, it addresses itself to contemporary problems. (It is not always understood how much of Tennyson's poetry is contemporary in theme and mood, despite his longing for the past.) 'Audley Court' includes a Theocritean song contest between the two young men who spend the day together. 'The Golden Year' is a further development of this mode, in that the song of the poet Leonard is answered not by another song, but by James's prose (rendered of course in the blank verse which is the medium of the poem), and that both are put in doubt by a third voice, which is that of the explosion in the quarry, and its echoes.

The speaker tells his listener (who like him remains nameless) of the day he spent in Wales with Leonard and old James. He had made fun of Leonard, telling him he was out of touch with the modern world. Leonard replied that he had been born too late, that in this new age everything had already been done, but nevertheless gave him his song. The song was about the golden year or age which will surely come to man; an age of equal wealth and happiness, to which the spread of enlightenment and Christianity and free trade all look forward. But it ended on a note of despair, and old James answered this angrily, dismissing the whole concept of the song. For James, the visions of golden years are foolish dreaming. He broke his stick in anger, telling Leonard that in this age we must live in the present, and that the only hope is in work. Just as he finished, there was an explosion from the slate quarry higher up the mountain, and a series of great echoes.

NOTES AND GLOSSARY:

Wales: Wales is famous for its poetry, in Welsh and English, and preserves a long tradition of instruction in poetry. Tennyson, like Hopkins, studied the forms of Welsh poetry; the riddling triplets of Merlin in 'The Coming of Arthur' echo the triads of the Welsh bards

Snowdon: the highest mountain in Wales. Mountains are traditionally places where men may meet gods. In the last book of *The Prelude* of Wordsworth there is an ascent of Snowdon, and a vision

half way up: the fact that they are only halfway up the mountain may be significant, as a comment on modern poetry. Leonard's song is not brilliant as poetry, though whether or not Tennyson intended this is hard to say

the feverous days: that is, the modern times of feverish money-getting. The reference is to the Bible, Proverbs 30:15

count . . . herd: do not think me one of the vulgar masses

taken by the forelock: compare the saying 'take time by the forelock' (the hair growing just above the brow), meaning, do not let chance slip

ellipse: regular oval

returning on: repeating

Ah, though . . . flower: the slight undercurrent of a reservation about poetry is characteristic of the disappointed Leonard, and of Tennyson, of whom Leonard in some respects is a mocking self-portrait

When wealth: the image is that of mountain snow that, melting, waters the valleys. Tennyson may have been thinking of a sentence in Francis Bacon's essay, 'Of Seditions and Troubles', which occurs in a similar context: 'Money is like muck, not good except it be spread'

man be liker man: that is, be more like his glorious origins and real self

Shall eagles . . . : although man will be enlightened and prosperous, he will not be dull; there will still be degrees of excellence. The falcon is a lesser bird of prey than the eagle. The emblematic nature of the eagle and wren antithesis (the wren is a tiny bird) suggests the riddling of the old Welsh triads

the Press: normally the newspapers, but here printing in general, and so literacy and information

oaken stock: stump or main trunk of the oak tree, which is known for its strength, here covered over but not subdued by the hoary (or white) clematis

stuff: nonsense. Note the angry brevity of the phrases that follow

God love us: a mild oath

rapt / Upon: lost in a vision of

He spoke: a phrase typical of epic, and so of idyll's use of older forms. See 'So said he' ('Morte d'Arthur', l.265)

them: the unseen workmen, busy while others talk

flap . . . buffet . . . bluff . . . bluff: the onomatopoeia is comparable with that of the last two lines of 'Come down, O maid'. It is not decoration in either case, though critics have sometimes thought that it was. The dramatic emphasis here is on pure sound resulting from action, as distinct from words. To flap is to strike lightly with something broad, often used of the movement of a large bird's wing; to buffet (archaic) is to strike with the hand; a bluff is a headland with a perpendicular broad face

---

From *Maud* (1855)

Part I, iii

The hero and narrator of the monodrama speaks of the beauty of the young girl Maud, whom he knew as a child. She is the daughter of the man who helped ruin his father, and may have caused his death, probably by suicide. When Maud and her brother return to the neighbouring Hall, he is thinking of leaving his lonely home on the moor, and going abroad. Seeing her as her carriage passed, he found fault with her beauty. Now he realises that she fascinates him. The poem is perhaps Tennyson's finest sonnet; the other outstanding sonnet is 'The Kraken', of 1830. The effect of the single period and long lines is that of a fascination he has fought against, and which he suddenly realises has overcome him. There is no division between octave and sestet, and the rhyme scheme (*ababcdbcdbdebe*) is a skilful variation on more traditional sonnet rhymes: the dominant *b* rhyme, with its deep '-ound' note, invades the second quatrain, recurs just after it, in 1.10, and in 1.13 intrudes between 'wave' and 'grave' in such a way as to modify the effect of a closing couplet. Like much of Tennyson's poetry, this has to do with a passive subject, which is the speaker; the repeated participles of 'growing and fading and growing' are stronger than the verbs 'arose,' 'walked,' and even 'found,' in spite of the strength of its *b* rhyme.

NOTES AND GLOSSARY:

clear-cut:	suggests sculpture, and classic beauty
cruelly meek:	a bitter paradox
spleenful:	'spleen' means ill-humour or peevishness, and often a settled mood in which one rejects the world and humankind
dead on the cheek:	the movement to this line from 'her eyes were downcast' in the previous section (l.5), where he remembers actually seeing her, shows the growing passion; this detail is significant
pale:	a pale complexion was for long regarded as desirable in women
Womanlike:	implying a rejection of women, which is part of his spleen
a transient wrong:	that is, the fault he found (or tried to find) with her beauty, in I, ii
growing upon me:	taking possession of me
ground:	land surface. We speak of a house and its 'grounds'; at the same time there is, as elsewhere in *Maud* (I, xi), an attempt to feel solid ground
now to ... Now to:	the movement is of the waves, now flung up the beach, now dragging back the pebbles as they retire
wintry ... daffodil dead:	the effect is that of strange season between winter and spring
Orion:	a constellation

Part I, x, stanzas 1 and 2
He has met Maud (in I, vi), and his recognition of her truth and kindly

'womanhood' has made the world less bitter. But later (I, ix) he has seen her riding on the moor with two men, one of whom was probably her arrogant older brother, and the other the weakling whom the brother approves as her suitor. His suspicions return, and with them his bitterness about the corrupt state of mercantile and industrial England, and his own weaknesses. The verse, like much of the verse in *Maud*, is trochaic (/ ⌣), and its roughness, and the plainness of the language, is that of the angry voice concerned now only with what he sees as the bitter truth.

NOTES AND GLOSSARY:

new-made lord: Tennyson had some respect for the old aristocracy, but none for what amounts to a bought peerage

blacker pit: presumably Hell. Tennyson had in fact no belief in eternal punishment

trams: coal-trucks underground were dragged by men and women, often naked in the heat

simper: this, and what follows, does not follow grammatically from the phrase 'that all men adore'; the effect is that of angry speech, careless of correct constructions

gewgaw: gaudy and valueless. Tennyson probably had in mind the preposterous house built by the Tennyson d'Eyncourts

perky: the sense is of something small, spirited, and impudent. Probably the trees were newly planted

the sullen-purple moor: rather like Hardy's Egdon Heath, in its indifference to man

Look at it: the parenthetical and contemptuous growl is typical of the tone

cockney: at that time, the word usually meant the new and vulgar gentility of the suburbs. The pricking or cocking of the ear suggests a vulgar alertness

padded shape: the use of padding and corsets for men was not uncommon even in the early twentieth century: coat-shoulders, of course, are still padded. 'Shape' means 'figure'

bought commission: the practice of buying a commission, or the rank of an army officer, was still common. It was defended on the grounds that fully professional officers of any social rank or origin would constitute a dangerous force within the kingdom. Tennyson sees the practice as corruption

rabbit mouth: projecting rabbit-like front teeth are sometimes thought to be a characteristic feature of the English governing classes

splenetic: from 'spleen'

to the heart of life: the sense is stronger than 'sick to the heart' or 'sick of life'

Part I, xviii, stanzas 1, 2, and 3

The central love poem in *Maud*; the first three stanzas, which Tennyson said could be read as one, are one of the great love poems of the language. Maud has confessed her love for him, and, as he says in wonder (in stanza 6), 'it seems that I am happy'. The opening line is a variation on the dominant theme of the marriage hymns which celebrate the leading home of the bride. It is to her own home, the Hall, that he leads her, though one or two critics have mistakenly thought otherwise. (Maud has done no more than tell him that she loves him.) In the wide range of styles in *Maud*, nothing is more impressive than the Hebraic or biblical style of the opening two lines, and the repetition of the Hebraic second line at the beginning of the second and third stanzas, against the iambics, which are not characteristic of the mono-drama. (By 'Hebraic,' of course, is meant the style of the English Authorised Version of the early seventeenth century, the rhythms of which are everywhere in English poetry.) This may have influenced Tennyson in the passage on the cedar of Lebanon outside the Hall, which echoes the Psalms of David, and by which the experience of love is returned to its origin in the thornless Garden of Eden.

NOTES AND GLOSSARY:

the long-wished-for end: this passage, among others elsewhere, makes nonsense of the suggestion by some critics that Maud has already yielded to him as her lover. He is a man of honour, however unbalanced, and would hardly have taken advantage of a sixteen-year-old girl in the temporary absence of her brother

pattering: onomatopoeic, like rain falling, or rapid idle talk

The gates ... Heaven: the exaggeration is that of a supreme moment of emotion

Lebanon ... cedar: the cedars of Lebanon are spoken of in the Bible, Psalm 104: 16

made ... altar-flame: his life is now one of adoration and service, not only to Maud, but to truth

forefathers: the reference is to the trees of the Garden of Eden

Part I, xx

One of the most frequently misunderstood sections. He is so happy that he is light-headed, and fears nothing. But Maud (usually dismissed by critics as a shadowy figure) sees more clearly, young though she is. She knows that her brother, although not such a brute as the hero believes, is dangerous, and foresees some disaster. He does not understand the reasons for her melancholy, suggesting others. The dramatic verse of the first part ambles along at the easy pace of the hero's confident misapprehensions. Its feminine, or unstressed, endings, and the complacent rhyming prattle about Maud's two dresses, express his delighted condescension to her. The condescension is both masculine, and born of the fact that he is nine years older than her. (Maud, incidentally, is still 'maiden Maud,' though it is hardly worth mentioning.) He passes from this to a sarcastic description of the political dinner and ball which her brother will give tomorrow, to which he has not, of course, been invited. At the end of the dancing, however, he will wait for Maud in her rose-garden.

NOTES AND GLOSSARY:

I:	that is, instead of Maud trying to lighten his habitual melancholy, he is trying to lighten her mood
The Sultan:	the nickname they have given her brother, with his arrogant authority. There are several echoes in *Maud* of the *Arabian Nights*, a collection of Oriental folk tales dating from the tenth century
worldly:	Maud's brother has been telling her of the need to make a wealthy marriage
a little lazy lover:	that is, the rabbit-faced lord, of whom he is now able to think with some indulgence. At least one critic (Paull Baum) has mistakenly thought that the brother is reproving Maud for not paying enough attention to the hero
his caresses:	this is figurative
pronounce upon:	make a judgment
habit:	riding-habit or dress
gipsy bonnet:	wide-brimmed hat
if we live:	if God spares us; the phrase is sarcastic
ponderous squire:	the squire was usually the local landlord, and a man of some power; its use here is sarcastic ('ponderous' means heavy and slow-moving), as is that of 'squirelings' or little squires
titmouse:	tit, or small bird
grand political dinner:	note the mocking repetition of this phrase in 1.31
the Tory:	the right-wing and landowning interest; 'the' is a mocking reference to the Tory as a *genus* or breed. An election is coming, and Maud's brother is standing for office; the political dinner is part of his campaign, and the ball is part of the marriage-market, to ensure the continuance of the Tory

all as well delighted: just as pleased (as if I had been invited)
Your glory also: Maud in her jewels and ball-gown. This is probably
                        a coming-out ball for Maud, when girls of mar-
                        riageable age were formally introduced into society
render / All homage: pay formal honour (note 'Queen Maud')

Part I, xxii

An expression of the narrator's ecstasy as he waits for Maud in her
garden. This is the last section of Part I, and is followed by the catastrophe of the fatal duel with her brother, and their separation, in Part
II. The verse and stanza forms throughout are regular, with some inter-
esting variations. The falling or trochaic measure ($\diagdown\smile$) characteristic of   ⌐7
the monodrama is reversed to a rapid anapaestic: $\smile\smile\diagup$. Ruskin drew
attention to Tennyson's mastery of the verse forms, showing that not
one line is exactly similar to another in its prosody. The rose and the lily
are at the heart of the dominant flower imagery. These classic images
of passion and purity which mingle here occur elsewhere in *Maud*,
though the common critical belief that the symbols have more weight
than the action is unfounded; the symbolism of *Maud* is not complex.
The rhythm also evokes the music of the ballroom. The poem was set
to music by Balfe, and out of its context became a popular drawing-
room song. The reversal of the movement in the last stanza, discussed
in Part 3, is perhaps the most brilliant effect of the poem.

NOTES AND GLOSSARY:
a breeze of morning: Cf. *In Memoriam* 95 (xcv), ll.53−61
the planet of Love: the morning star Venus, or Phosphorus
faint: as the light of the sun grows; the metaphor of
                         ll.9−12 is sexual
half: that is, half of the departing guests
young lord-lover: Maud's official wooer; as in I, xx, he can now
                         afford to speak of him without rancour
clashed: usually suggests a harsh discordant noise: here it
                         probably signifies a contrast between the garden of
                         growing things, and the loud noise from the ball-
                         room. Note 'hall', not 'Hall'; that is, the ballroom,
                         not the house
Our wood: the wood near his house, where he walks with
                         Maud
would not shake: because there had been no breeze
start: make a sudden involuntary movement
purple and red: imperial colours of triumph; also suggesting blood

Part II, v, stanzas 1, 2, 3, 4, 6, 9, 10, 11

In II, i, we learn that Maud's brother, with the young lord, found them at
the gate, and insulted them. The brother fell in the duel that followed;

the hero fled to France, where he learnt of Maud's death. Haunted by what he thinks is her phantom, he returns to London. This section is spoken in a madhouse, in which he has been confined. In his madness he believes that he has died and has been buried, but cannot find peace even in the grave. (At the end of I, i, when we first meet him, he wants to reject the world, and bury 'myself in myself': in a sense, he has now done that.) The verse, like that of several other sections, has a rough fluency, as his diseased mind hurries from one obsession to another. This was always inherent in *Maud*, whose original subtitle was 'The Madness'. The section returns to the disgust with a corrupt and murderous society with which *Maud* began.

NOTES AND GLOSSARY:

Dead:	that is, Maud
the wheels:	in the previous section he spoke of the continual 'roaring of the wheels' in London
only a yard:	see Dickens for descriptions of choked city cemeteries, in *Bleak House, A Christmas Carol*, and elsewhere
Driving . . . burying:	the meaningless jostle of life; see 'the noise of life' in *In Memoriam* 7 (VII)
is that not sad?:	typical of the darting changes in the intonation
tithes:	produce or money paid to the Church, voluntarily or as a tax
A touch of their office:	the slightest exercise of their function
fain would:	would be glad to
us:	the madmen, whom he thinks of as dead, like himself
tickle the maggot:	'maggot', or larva to be found in decaying organic matter, here has its old meaning of a fancy or whim
the prophecy:	obscure. It may be the prophecy in the Bible, Luke 12:3, that 'Whatsoever ye have spoken in darkness shall be heard in the light, and that which ye have spoken in the ear in closets shall be proclaimed upon the housetops'; see below
closet:	small private room
***him*:**	probably Maud's brother
poison our babes:	this is a reminiscence of I, i, l.45, where he refers to the poisoning of children by poor parents to avoid paying money to burial-societies
the old man:	Maud's father, who he believes brought about his own father's death
a pit:	the pit in which the body of his father was found, and in which the duel was fought; see I, i and II, i. The image recurs in *Maud*

a friend of mine: that is, his father

the Quaker: popular name for a member of the Christian sect, the Society of Friends; the reference is to their refusal to sanction killing

---

'Northern Farmer: New Style' (1869)

One of the dialect poems Tennyson wrote in later life; a companion poem to 'Northern Farmer: Old Style', where a dying farmer stoically faces death, and recalls, with much else, how he cleared a notorious stretch of waste land. The dialect is from the north of England. The new-style farmer is intent on 'proputty' (property). His son Sam has fallen in love with the parson's daughter; since the parson is poor, the rich farmer disapproves. He tells Sam he is a fool, and having laid down the law on love and marriage, he informs him that if he does not marry wisely (that is, for money), he will disinherit him in favour of Dick, who is presumably the younger son. Some of this is said while they are driving briskly on the highway, some (xi–xiv) while the father is sitting in the gig or trap waiting for Sam to break a stick for the horse.

NOTES AND GLOSSARY:

Dosn't: doesn't

thou, tha: characteristic Northern dialect usage

'ear, 'erse: hear, horse. In dialect initial 'h' and 'th' are often dropped (as ''em' for 'them'), as are final 'n' and 'f' ('i'' for 'in,' 'o'' for 'of')

canters: between a trot and a gallop, an easy three-beat movement

awaäy: characteristic Northern vowel lengthening

proputty: property; note the three-beat sound of the hooves

for thy paaïns: that is, all your efforts are for nothing

moor: more

nor: (*dialect*) than

Woä: 'woa' is the cry which stops or slows a horse

a craw to pluck: to have a crow to pluck or a bone to pick means to have a reason to quarrel

a man or a mouse: the habitual plain man's contempt for the parson and his books

to weeäk: (*dialect*) this week

let ma 'ear mysén speäk: presumably to the horse ('mysén' means 'myself')

Thou'll not marry for munny: sarcastic

sweet upo': in love with

parson's lass: the daughter ('lass' also means 'girl') of the clergy-man or (as here) the curate

Saäints-daäy: a day in the Church calendar commemorating a saint

soä is scoors o' gells: so are scores of girls; 'so' is characteristically lengthened; third person plural 'is' occurs in many dialects

the flower as blaws: the flower that blooms (blows)

sticks: remains

stunt: (*dialect*) obstinate

towd: told

coom to 'and: came to hand, or became available

laaïd by: laid by, or saved

nicetish: nice, in the sense of good, adequate

thowt: thought

cuddle: hug

'ant nowt: hasn't nothing (the double negative is dialect usage)

guvness: the usual profession of poor unmarried educated women was that of governess

addle: (*dialect*) earn

nobbut: nothing but

curate: the underpaid parish priest's assistant

git hissen clear: get himself clear (of poverty or debt)

ligs: (*dialect*) lies. There is a proverb which says that you must lie on your bed as you have made it

shere: shire, or county

Varsity: university. Poor undergraduates could easily get into debt by imitating rich undergraduates, and betting on horses. If the debt had to be taken up at high interest, they could spend the rest of their lives paying it

Stook: stuck

i' the grip: (*dialect*) in the ditch

noän: none

·shuvv: shove

a far-weltered yowe: a hopelessly overturned ewe (female sheep), which is unable to rise because of the weight of its fleece

reäson why: that's the reason (a most smug complacent remark)

burn: born (Class prejudice: what is Sammy up to, mixing with the gentry?)

an ass as near as mays nowt: this parenthesis is about the parson, a fool who makes (earns) little or nothing

dangtha:	damn you
the bees is as fell as owt:	the flies are as fierce as anything
esh:	ash (tree known for its straight growth)
'oop yonder:	up there (in heaven). Those who have property do not rob and steal, so presumably go to Heaven
loomp:	lump (taken as a whole). The line is a most bitter comment by Tennyson on the morality of the moneyed classes
feythers:	fathers
mun 'a gone to the gittin':	must have gone to (been needed for) the getting, or earning
ammost:	almost
leästways:	at least (Perhaps he means that if his father had any money, he himself never saw it)
tued and moiled:	(*dialect*) toiled and drudged
a good 'un:	a good one; that is, rich
'e did:	confirmatory
beck:	(*dialect*) brook
Feyther run oop:	'run' for 'ran'; that is, his land
noätions:	notions, ideas (an understatement)
wheerby:	whereby, usually by/because of which, here meaning 'to which'

'Frater Ave atque Vale' (1883)

This exquisite poem records a visit to the ruins of the house of the Roman poet Catullus (?84–?54 BC) at Sirmio, on Lake Garda in Italy. (Actually the 'Roman ruin' is that of a later building than the villa of Catullus, but Tennyson did not know this.) It alludes to two poems by Catullus, one on a visit to his brother's tomb in Asia Minor, and one on his happy return to his house after a long voyage. 'Atque in perpetuum, frater, ave atque vale,' from Catullus's poem about his dead brother, means 'and for ever, brother, hail and farewell'. 'O venusta Sirmio' ('O lovely Sirmio') is from the second poem, as are some of the phrases in the last two lines. The metre is Tennyson's favourite metre of eight-foot trochaics, with the last foot catalectic, or cut from / ⌣ to /. Notice how the poem begins and ends with 'us' and 'we', and contains an individual sorrow: 'to me', in l.3. Tennyson visited Sirmio with his son Hallam, and remembered the recent death of his brother Charles.

NOTES AND GLOSSARY:

your Sirmione:	the Italian, not the Latin name; probably used by the boatmen whom he addresses, hence the playful 'your Sirmione'
ruin ... flowers:	a classic image of death and life

Lydian laughter:	taken from Catullus, referring to the laughter of the bright waves. The old Etruscan inhabitants of the region were said to be descended from the Lydians of Asia Minor
all-but-island:	Sirmione is a peninsula; Tennyson's 'all-but-island' is a close rendering of Catullus's 'paene insularum', and gives something of the immediacy of the Latin as it would sound to a Latin speaker
olive-silvery:	the silvery underside of the olive leaves shows when the wind blows. The wind is a symbol of life, and as often in Tennyson's late short poems, life seems stronger than death, even here

---

'To E. Fitzgerald' (1885)

Lines 1−56 are an epistolary poem or verse letter to Tennyson's old friend Edward Fitzgerald (1809−83), known to him as 'Fitz'. In 1859 Fitzgerald published his famous translation from the Persian, *The Rubáiyát of Omar Khayyám*. Fitzgerald died before receiving the birthday poem. In ll.46−62 Tennyson refers to his early unpublished poem 'Tiresias'. When he published 'To E. Fitzgerald', ll.1−56 appeared as an introduction to 'Tiresias', and ll.57−88, on Fitzgerald's death, as epilogue. The poem is written in unseparated quatrains, and the introduction is of a single period; the leisurely accumulation of intimate and tender memories is interrupted by death. It is one of the finest of the late epistolary poems, and its urbanity, wit, and perfect ease recall Latin Augustan poets such as Horace (65−8 BC).

NOTES AND GLOSSARY:

tarried:	lingered
Orb of change:	a preoccupation of Tennyson's. 'Orb' means a celestial body, especially the earth or sun
your diet spares:	Fitzgerald was a vegetarian

Whatever moved . . . prayers: the reference is to the Bible, Acts 10: 11−12, and to the animals lowered to Peter for food, in a vessel, 'as it had been a great sheet knit at the four corners'

table of Pythagoras: Pythagoras (?580−?500BC) was a Greek philosopher and mathematician, who advocated vegetarianism because he believed that the transmigration of souls, or passing of souls from one body to another at death, included those of animals as well as men

'a thing enskied': 'a thing enskied and sainted / By your renouncement − an immortal spirit' (Shakespeare, *Measure for Measure* I.iv.34−5)

flashed in frost: the stars shine more brightly when there is frost
that wholesome heat: healthy heat; the effect of eating meat
set: started
there rolled / To meet me: he is describing a dream
Eshcol: see the Bible, Numbers 13:23; the men sent by Moses to search the land of Canaan, which the Lord had given to the children of Israel, brought back a huge bunch of grapes from the brook of Eshcol
Lenten: Lent is a period of fasting and penance before Easter
lay: (*archaic*) poem, that is, the *Rubáíyát*
cast it: threw it off
large infidel: 'large' includes the sense of 'large-souled'; the picture given in the *Rubáíyát* is of a man who is in no sense a puritan. There is a gentle irony in 'infidel', since this follower of Islam seems to have loved wine
plaudits: applause
Two voices: those of James Spedding and W.H. Brookfield, two old Cambridge friends
seventy-five: Fitzgerald was actually seventy-four when he died
Less for its own: less for its own sake than mine, who recall gracious times
'One height . . . fire': from the last line of 'Tiresias': 'On one far height in one far-shining fire'
opulent: Fitzgerald did not admire much of Tennyson's poetry after the 1842 volumes, thinking it too decorative
over nice: too fastidious
Pagan Paradise: the reference (which the next line clarifies) is to the introduction's classic (and classical) celebration of cultured friendship, resembling those which, in the absence of a Christian concept of immortality, seem to have been as near felicity as the pagan Latin writers could approach
If night, what barren toil to be: that is, if death is only night, life is barren toil, or useless labour
with him: a last suggestion of companionship

Part 3

Commentary

The poems

Tennyson's juvenile and unfinished works, 'The Devil and the Lady' and 'Armageddon', were written two or three years after the death of Keats in 1821, and Shelley in 1822. Although dates alone prove little, the fact is worth remembering, to prevent us from thinking that the great Victorian poets are separated by many years from the younger Romantics. But the differences of thought and mode are great. Among the most characteristic works of the English Romantics are *The Prelude*, 'Kubla Khan', and *Prometheus Unbound*. In the first, the 'work of glory', or the long philosophical poem which haunted the Romantic poets, changes to doubt and uncertainty in Wordsworth's hands, and he turns from it to charting the early struggles of his mind to deal with the mysterious world of things. In the short 'Kubla Khan' of Coleridge, the world of action, in the great Khan who built the mighty dome, is in a sense superseded by the dream of the act of the poetic imagination, by which the dome might be built in air by song. Shelley's magnificent *Prometheus Unbound* is a continuation of the *Prometheus Bound* of the Greek dramatist Aeschylus, in which the mind regenerates itself by an act of will, and overcomes the tyrant which it has created, and by which it has been enslaved. This drama is basically a single symbolic act, and succeeds as the unfinished *Hyperion* of Keats probably could not have done. So far as we can understand, *Hyperion*, which Keats abandoned, was to have been a brief epic expressing the evolutionary idea of 'the eternal law / That first in beauty should be first in might'. Although it is the most intellectual of Keats's poems, it is difficult to see how the epic mode of extended narrative could have expressed this, as Shelley's lyric drama embodied the single act of regeneration. Although Wordsworth confronted the mysteries of being virtually without myth, Shelley and Keats returned to an earlier mode of apprehension in their adaptation and creation of myth, such as those of Prometheus and Jupiter, Apollo and Hyperion. With the Victorian poets, the great vision and the optimism of the imaginative constructions largely disappear, and so does the unitary or single structure.

The characteristic long poetic works of the later nineteenth century are *In Memoriam* and *Idylls of the King* of Tennyson, *The Ring and the Book* of Browning, and *Modern Love* of Meredith. The structure of *In Memoriam* and *Modern Love* is respectively that of a sequence of short elegies, and sonnets; that of *Idylls of the King* and *The Ring and the Book* of a series of idylls, and monologues. In place of the great mythic forms of *Prometheus Unbound*, there is the immediacy of individual experience. Of course regeneration in *The Prelude* is also highly individual, as individual as the operation of the symbols of mountain and stream, light and mist in the last book, which make up a vision or 'perfect image of a mighty Mind', and which are probably as near as Wordsworth can come to myth. But Wordsworth's poem is unusual in being the story of a poet's mind. The immediacy of the experience in *In Memoriam* is less that of a uniquely gifted mind, than that of a type of the human race, bearing down loss and fear by will, and with the help of time. Meredith's *Modern Love* gives the actuality of a failed marriage, a dilemma bitterly defined by the sardonic evocation of older stylistic modes. In *The Ring and the Book*, as G.K. Chesterton said, it is as if Browning had proposed to show us the relations of man to heaven, not through a great legend of love and war, like Homer, or by telling us of the very beginning of all things, like Milton, but by telling a story out of a book of criminal trials from which he has selected one of the meanest and most completely forgotten. The moments of vision are subordinated to the processes of the everyday, and the older and larger forms, which briefly triumphed again with the rejection of the scientific enlightenment of the eighteenth century, have disappeared.

English nineteenth-century poetry proposes less than the poetry of the English Romantics, and, as has been said by one critic, may in a sense be regarded as a domestication of Romantic poetry. In the rediscovered power of the unconscious and the irrational, these poets had triumphed over the enlightenment. But the Romantic poets' Victorian successors had to contend with a science which now immeasurably extended space and time, and with a society which had lost nearly all semblance of a centre. The popular idea of the Victorians as a race of overfed ladies and gentlemen complacently armoured in Scripture and banknotes is misleading. For one thing, financial speculation was rife, and there were frequent collapses. The signs of a world out of joint were everywhere. What the Victorians had to contend with was modernity, a world which was changing at a frightening pace. They were obsessed with the rawness of modern society, and with the bleak realities of man as a creature lost in space and time. They were haunted by the idea of an age when life had been otherwise, and looked back to the Middle Ages as a time when man was more than a speck of dust in space, or a unit in the minds of statisticians. But there were no great myths by which reality could be comprehended. The *Idylls of the King* uses only the accessories of medieval romance, to show the decline of civilisation, and the myth of evolution towards the divine that persists throughout the century (articulated briefly in *The Princess*, at length in *In Memoriam*) is shadowy, a matter of earnest hopes and glimpses.

The medium of modern revivals of myth is often vision. When Keats rehandles *Hyperion* as *The Fall of Hyperion*, he introduces it to the England of 1819 as a vision. 'Methought I stood where trees of every clime': it is at once here and everywhere, the whole held in the challenge of 'methought'. In either version he has his eye on what is to come, although he was to abandon *Hyperion*. But Tennyson's unfinished visionary poem 'Armageddon', largely written when he was fifteen, breaks off before the great battle of Armageddon itself. It is as if his only purpose is to declare himself a visionary poet, without giving the vision which would confirm it. Perhaps the last battle between Good and Evil was simply too much for the young Tennyson's powers. But the choice of theme suggests that from the beginning it was only a formality.

> I felt my soul grow godlike, and my spirit
> With supernatural excitation bound
> Within me, and my mental eye grew large
> With such a vast circumference of thought,
> That, in my vanity, I seemed to stand
> Upon the outward verge and bound alone
> Of God's omniscience.

This, the capacity rather than the act, is what concerns him: 'Yea! in that hour I could have fallen down / Before my own strong soul and worshipped it'. It is comparable in its way to much of the substance of Browning's early poem *Paracelsus* (1835). Youthful ambition plays its part in all this, of course, but the insistence on the creative mind seems to push into the background what the mind must create. In 'Timbuctoo' (1829), with which Tennyson won the Chancellor's Gold Medal at Cambridge, and which is largely an adaptation of 'Armageddon', the celebration of 'all that makes the wondrous mind of Man' is paradoxically both countered and confirmed by the speech of the Spirit of Fable, who in 'Armageddon' had been the young seraph inspiring the visionary with godlike powers. On the one hand, exploration will reveal the great fabled city of Timbuctoo as a squalid mud-walled settlement. On the other, the great power of Fable is 'deep-rooted in the living soil of truth'. That is, the scientific mind destroys fable, as Keats argued Newton had destroyed the rainbow, yet mind still shadows forth the Unattainable. Tennyson thought 'Timbuctoo' was 'a wild and unmethodized performance', and indeed there is a notable difference between what the Spirit of Fable says about himself and man, and what he says about the loss of Timbuctoo, his latest throne.

Tennyson derived something of this from Wordsworth's considera-
tion of fable and Greek mythology in *The Excursion* (IV, 631–940),
which inspired Keats to take up what Wordsworth had virtually rejected. Coleridge has a memorable passage on the death of fable, in his
translation of *The Piccolomini* of the German poet Friedrich von Schiller (1759–1805). (The passage, II.4.1·19–38, enlarges on the original,
and indeed is almost as much Coleridge as Schiller.) Fable 'delightedly
believes / Divinities, being himself divine'; the old intelligible forms

> live no longer in the faith of reason!
> But still the heart doth need a language, still
> Doth the old instinct bring back the old names.

The old names of Hera, Pallas Athena, and Aphrodite (Juno, Minerva
and Venus are the Roman counterparts) appear in Tennyson's
'Oenone' (1832 and 1842), but less as myth than as a group in some
characteristic Renaissance painting of the famous Judgment of Paris.
Aphrodite appears several times in his poetry: a single magnificent
simile in *The Princess* (VII, 147–54); a near and dangerous presence,
partly divine, partly the process of generation, in 'Lucretius'; a distant
but no less dangerous presence in 'Tithonus'. In general, the poems in
which Tennyson uses or creates myth are brief, and the myth is often
highly personal. That of 'The Lady of Shalott' is more ample than
most; significantly, it has to do with the problem of the artist who must
and must not remain apart from a society which fears him. Tennyson's
source was an old Italian story; nearly everything which he added to it
– the tapestry, the mirror, the island – is what makes the poem a myth
of the isolation of the modern artist. The myth of 'Tithonus' is more
private. As 'Tithon' (1833) – it was not published, in an extended and
improved form, until 1860 – it was a companion poem to 'Ulysses'. In
Greek myth Tithonus was the mortal lover of Aurora, goddess of the
dawn, who gave him eternal life, but not eternal youth. Now he lies
eternally withering in her arms, in the gleaming halls of morning, beg-
ging to be returned to the cycle of generation from which he impiously
broke free, so that he may rest in death. A minor myth becomes an
embodiment of Tennyson's fear of mortality, and sense of loss.

It is one of the finest of his poems, and is a perfect example of the
strengths and limitations of his myth-making. It is very far indeed from
the symbolism of Shelley's lyric drama, and Keats's projected epic. No
law is affirmed for man, no great action is undertaken. A mortal sickness, or sickness of mortality, a single desolate state of soul, is trans-
lated by the myth into a state between mortal and immortal, from
which the only release – that of death – is denied. Without fable, Tennyson could hardly have achieved the strange authority of this death in
life. What is interesting is the use he makes of fable. The use he made

of the very brief episode of the Lotos-Eaters in Homer's *Odyssey* is in a way similar. This becomes a legend of world-weariness and withdrawal from care, so exquisitely sung that the drugged sloth almost frees itself from the Homeric narrative, in which the sailors are brought back to the ship. Withdrawal, of one sort or another, is the common theme of all three poems, and, in its own way, of 'Ulysses'. It sometimes seems that only this, and then only intermittently, could move Tennyson to the creation of myth.

But the whole of his life, as man and poet, was not in withdrawal, and the satiric monologue 'St Simeon Stylites' need not be taken to mean a disgusted retreat from life. In satire the perception of human folly is sometimes sharpened by a strong appetite for life on the part of the satirist. Many of his own fears do appear in the poem, and the recurring fear that suicide might be the only release is the strongest of them. But Tennyson's contempt for selfish asceticism makes Simeon a feast for him. His friend Fitzgerald said that 'this was one of the Poems [he] would read with grotesque Grimness, especially at such passages as "Coughs, Aches, Stitches, etc." [ll.13–6], laughing aloud at times'. Since Simeon was canonised by the Church, he is a great type of human error. His sanctity is bought by his self-inflicted punishment for his supposed sinning, and the punishment is made grotesquely public. In his description of himself as being 'from scalp to sole one slough and crust of sin', sin and punishment are hardly to be distinguished. He calls himself 'A sign betwixt the meadow and the cloud', and in so doing says more than he knows: meadow and cloud are images of fertility, and suspended as he is between them, he is a sign of death. The folly and the self-deceit are squalid; the mastery by which we are made to take delight in them is unfaltering. Although there are passages in *Maud* and elsewhere which recall the peculiar force of the poem, Tennyson did not again achieve such satiric force, on such a scale.

The companion poems 'Northern Farmer: Old Style' and 'Northern Farmer: New Style' (1864 and 1869), in particular the second poem, are also satiric. The first deals with an age which is passing, when men subdued the wilderness, and looked to tradition. The second is of the new age of property. The old-style farmer reviews the past from his deathbed. He will still drink his ale, whatever the doctor says, because he will not break his rule. As for the parson who keeps telling him his duty, ''e reäds wonn sarmin a weeäk, an' I 'a stubbed Thurnaby waäste'. The stubbing, or clearing, of Thurnaby waste to make it into farmland is the great heroic effort of his life, and beside this the parson's one weekly sermon is matter for contempt. There was a ghost in the wasteland, which may or may not have been a 'butter-bump' or bittern (a bird with a loud booming cry), and the ghost was turned out with the rest of the rubbish. Perhaps his successor will use a steam-engine to work the land, but that he could not bear to see. It is the voice of the obstinate traditional peasant, unconcerned with spiritual values or fears. He has kept in mind his duty to the Squire, and now cannot imagine how Squire will get on without him; in fact, does God Almighty know what He is doing, in taking him to Himself? The new-style farmer, on the other hand, is bent on extending his 'proputty'. If his son disagrees, and marries for love rather than money, he is an ass. In place of the old complex and deep-rooted loyalties, there are merely those who have, and those who have not, and his view of the have-nots is simple: 'Taäke my word for it, Sammy, the poor in a loomp is bad'. Disraeli (1804–81), the conservative statesman and novelist, spoke in *Sybil* (1845) of the two Englands or two nations, of the rich and the poor; this is the voice of the newly rich, uncompromisingly defining their position.

Less powerful than 'St Simeon Stylites' though they are, the grasp of these two poems on major contemporary issues is sure: Tennyson saw the changes and the dangers as clearly as any novelist of his time. Withdrawal and absence are potent forces in his poetry, but in fact he withdrew from the issues of contemporary life as little as Browning. The nakedness of nineteenth-century man is nowhere more apparent than in the dream of section 70 (LXX) of *In Memoriam*, where the city crowds of industrial man mingle with the strange beasts on the shores of a prehistoric world.

And crowds that stream from yawning doors,
  And shoals of puckered faces drive;
  Dark bulks that tumble half alive,
And lazy lengths on boundless shores.

But this is a sudden vision of the world as it seems to a man oppressed by modern society, and the conclusions of modern science. Elsewhere the modern world, with its momentary securities, its social changes, and uncertain future, is less a weight than something lived in, a local habitation for the abiding concerns of poetry. The fluttering of the flame under the tea-urn in *In Memoriam*, 95 (XCV) may seem unpoetic, a minor domestic detail, yet it too presages what is to come. The marriage which ends the sequence is of its time, with its champagne and white-favoured horses. In 'The Golden Year', as we have seen, the older forms and language of the poet Leonard, sung on the mountain where according to legend men and gods may meet, and looking uncertainly to some future good, yield to the modern ethic of present work and present good of James, who resembles the historian and political philosopher Thomas Carlyle (1795–1881). Both in turn yield to the blast from the slate-quarry, where the nameless workers ('I heard them') are shaping present and future without words or theories.

This is one of the 'English Idyls' (he tended to use the spelling 'idyll' for *The Idylls of the King*) which are among his most characteristic poems. The word 'idyll' derives from a Greek word meaning a little picture, and tends to mean a poem giving a single image of life in such a way as to suggest that there is much more than it is willing to state directly. In his 'English Idyls' Tennyson follows the example of his beloved Theocritus, the Sicilian Greek poet of the third century BC. The poetry of Theocritus is very much of its age, which in some respects resembles the age of Tennyson as a cultured European would see it: a sophisticated age of material prosperity for many, and of easy communications and travel among nations; an age strongly conscious of its own modernity, and of the impossibility of recovering older forms and pieties. This is the age of Alexandrian poetry, of the Hellenistic culture that flourished in Alexandria in the last three centuries BC, with which English Victorian poetry is sometimes compared: at its best it followed principles of elaborate techniques, and was generally on a smaller scale than the poetry and drama of a heroic age. So in 'Audley Court' (1842) the old tradition of the song contest which Theocritus used is followed by Tennyson in a poem which subtly reflects the England of his day. The two young men sing of love and freedom, while picnicking in the grounds of Audley Court, the great house which has been sold, and passes now to a new proprietor. Although this is change, they seem timeless in their careless young manhood. But timeless though they seem, it is all in the past; the valediction on it in the last paragraph is 'So sang we to each other', and by what follows, the glad present he speaks of becomes memory. 'Walking to the Mail' (1842) is a rather bleak dialogue between John, a decent kindly man, and the jaundiced and complacent James. 'Mail' suggests the modern world of news and information and bustle. The substance of the poem is news or information about ourselves, in this England of the 1830s: the ghosts and devils that haunt us; class barriers, and unequal laws; fears of Chartist or workers' revolts; the England of the haves and the have-nots, the two Englands of Disraeli. On the one hand there is John's charity and integrity, on the other James's restricted and restricting 'sense of daily life', which enables one to keep one's head, and not go under. The poem is an experiment in the spareness of everyday speech. Its subtlety is that of what its statements half reveal: the pause near the end after John's oblique reproof to James, before he takes up the conversation again, is a case in point. We may find this more impressive than the return in the last few lines to the insistence on the richness and variety of the world as it appeared to John at the beginning of the poem; there is a slight element of contrivance in the poem, as if Tennyson were working to a formula.

Alert and accurate in its observation though it is, 'Walking to the Mail' is less typical of Tennyson than 'Audley Court', with the strong sense of the past which concludes that idyll. The elegiac *In Memoriam* is, of course, the monument to Tennyson's sense of what has been. The classic turn in elegy is that from grief to triumph – 'the dead are not dead but alive', as he says in 'Vastness' (1885) – which is found in the 'Lycidas' of John Milton (1608–74), the great poet of *Paradise Lost*, and in Shelley's 'Adonais'. But in *In Memoriam* there has never been any doubt of Hallam's immortality. (Even immortality is unequal; in 41 (XLI) he expresses the (to us) extraordinary fear that in the evolutionary stages of immortality, Hallam will always be ahead of him, and that he can never again be his equal.) The real elegiac turn or change in *In Memoriam* is a long swelling movement, rather than a turn, which is natural enough when one remembers its length: 'the glory of the sum of things' in 88 (LXXXVIII); the significant failure of the attempt to meet as spirit to spirit, and the renewal of life that follows, in 95 (XCV); the renewed Christ of 106 (CVI); the courageous acceptance of death, and life, in 107 (CVII); the understanding of the meaning of 'barren faith, / And vacant yearning' in 108 (CVIII):

> What find I in the highest place,
> But mine own phantom chanting hymns?
> And on the depths of death there swims
> The reflex of a human face.

But as has been said, it is a single poem only by courtesy, and the diary or confession-like structure sometimes indicates rather than embodies the mind working its way from stark grief, through speculation and hypotheses, to a form of faith.

It is personal, and exploratory. But it is sometimes the case with Tennyson's poetry (or indeed with anyone's poetry) that no sooner have we made a remark like that, than we must admit that a contrary is also true. For the intimate and personal in *In Memoriam* is sometimes found together with a rather impersonal language, which resembles that of English Augustan or eighteenth-century poetry. At its worst this can produce facile Augustan diction like 'the silver hair' in 84 (LXXXIV), l.32, which is so general that it is feeble. At its best, in lyrics like 9 (IX) or 17 (XVII), it goes back through the English Augustans to the Roman Augustan poet Horace: a phrase like 'the placid ocean-plains' from 9 (IX) has a long tradition behind it. In spite of several deprecating comments on the poetry itself (Prologue, ll.41–4; 48 (XLVIII); Epilogue, ll.21–4), one feels that in Tennyson's elegies the language itself is a means of achieving constancy. In this stylistic sense (as well as in the more obvious sense that these are poems, and not meant for a single day), the elegies go far beyond the diary or confession, and give substance to his remark, that 'it is rather the cry of the whole human race than mine'. The Augustanism generalises and stabilises personal experience, in an age which badly needed such stability. At the same time, it reflects a tendency in Tennyson to shrink from the world of things. His understanding of things is wonderfully expressed through sight and sound, but there is less sense of physical contact or identification than we find in many other poets, notably in Keats. As one critic has said, *In Memoriam* is a backward step from Wordsworth's *Prelude*, which was published in the same year, though it had been completed nearly fifty years before. Wordsworth's great passage about the Babe in II, 232−60 has to do with man's contact and kindred with the active universe. But Tennyson's section 45 (XLV) speaks of isolation from things as part of growth. The shrinking in this is the source of some of his greatest poetry, and the greatest poetry in the sequence has to do, on the whole, with fear and despair, rather than with triumph. It is also a source of some of the weakest poetry: the sometimes merely ornamental language, the unimpressive passages of domestic idyll, as in 6 (VI), or 40 (XL).

Maud was published five years later, in 1855, and took many of his admirers by surprise, causing indeed consternation in some quarters. In place of the gravity of *In Memoriam*, a strident and querulous voice was heard, raging against its disappointments, and anathematising the corruption of commercial England, with its financial speculations and its lies about peace, its marriage markets for the rich, and its poor huddled in their reeking sties. Tennyson's oddly protective attitude to this monodrama may be due to the fact that he projected something of himself into his neurotic hero. An unhappy love affair of the 1830s is probably reflected in it, and it is likely that the monodrama is in some respects cathartic, or cleansing, an attempt to rid himself of some of his unhappinesses and anxieties, or of the memory of them. Perhaps the stability of his position in the 1850s had something to do with this. *In Memoriam* had more than confirmed the reputation which the *Poems* of 1842 had begun, and by 1855 he was happily married. It is a fact that Tennyson was more protective about *Maud* than about anything else that he wrote. Always unwilling to hear criticism of his poetry, he regarded *Maud* as, in a peculiar sense, his child, and some of his contemporaries commented waspishly on his habit of subjecting visitors to long readings of it. On one occasion, Jane Carlyle, wife of Thomas Carlyle, heard him read *Maud*, and when he had finished said she thought it was '*stuff*'. Tennyson then read it through a second time, when she said she liked it a little better. Still unsatisfied, Tennyson read it to her a third time. The story is probably not greatly exaggerated.

The variety of its versification reflects the rapidly shifting moods of the unstable speaker, who goes mad after the death of his beloved Maud, and apparently recovers his sanity only by devoting himself to the national cause in the Crimean war with Russia. As has been suggested, it is an audaciously experimental work, and comparisons with eighteenth-century French melodrama, as a denial of Tennyson's originality, should be treated with caution. The twisted single vision of reality which it embodies is both a modern view, and a modern mode. Something of the progress of the monodrama can be seen from the scenes noted in Part 2. It starts with the hero alone in his house on the moor, raging against the corrupt age which has destroyed his father, calling for war, as more honourable than what is now called peace, and declaring his intention of burying himself in himself. With the appearance of Maud, whom he knew as a child and who is the daughter of the man who has ruined his father, this resolution is broken. He struggles against love, thinking her proud and hard, but yields to his recognition of her kindness. His fears return, with the appearance of a titled wooer of whom her arrogant brother seems to approve. This brother, who ignores him ('Gorgonized me [that is, turned me to stone] from head to foot / With a stony British stare') is now seen as the inheritor of the sin of Maud's family, who apparently ruined and rejected his family. It seems only Maud is pure, by some 'peculiar mystic grace' her mother's child only. In spite of all his suspicions and fears, she confesses her love for him, without her brother's knowledge. He passes into an ecstatic dream of happiness, looking forward eagerly to seeing her after the ball, in her rose-garden. Their meeting is interrupted by Maud's brother, with 'the babe-faced lord', who stands 'gaping and grinning by'. Harsh words are exchanged, and a blow is struck. The inevitable duel follows within the hour, in the pit or hollow where the body of the hero's father was found, and Maud's brother falls dying. Maud is stricken with grief, and the hero escapes to France, where he wanders in Brittany, tormented by remorse. He hears of Maud's death, and returns to London, oppressed by 'the roaring of the wheels', and 'the squares and streets, / And the faces that one meets, / Hearts with no love for me'. The end of the second part is,the famous madhouse scene, in which his old desire for burial finds strange expression, and in which the incidents of the story are distorted in his crazed mind.

The third and last part must be considered to be a failure. It is easy enough to see that Tennyson is trying to bring the wheel full circle, with the reminiscences in it of some of the early sections. It is possible to argue that although he said of his hero that he was now sane, though shattered, he is merely exchanging one obsession for another, with his desire to atone by taking part in what is presented as a national struggle against Russia. But although the sinking of his individuality in a national cause is typical of a modern tendency to simplify life by associating oneself with a national movement – a tendency to which the totalitarian régimes of the twentieth century bear witness – Tennyson's apparent willingness to believe in this solution suggests that there were things in *Maud* which were too close to him to be expressed even in a form of drama. Imperfect, technically dazzling, as firmly rooted in contemporary reality as in mental instability, *Maud* will always remain as typical of Tennyson in one way as *In Memoriam* is in another.

The tendency to suicide in *Maud* is strong, and its conclusion represents a kind of suicide, since the hero looks forward to his death as well as his service, as a form of atonement. Suicide, the death of the individual as a solution and release, is a recurring theme in Tennyson. The fullest statement of it is in 'The Two Voices' (1842). This describes a long night of anguish, in which 'a still small voice' argues for despair, and suicide, and is countered at last by the morning of hope, and the whispered encouragement of another voice. That the joyous natural scene with which it ends contains some rather pallid imitation of Wordsworth (it is an early poem, after all) is sometimes taken to indicate where Tennyson's deeper feelings lay. In the much later 'Lucretius' (1868), he takes up the story of the self-disgust of the great Roman poet, author of the *De Rerum Natura*, which ends in suicide, according to an old legend. The theme is present in 'Ulysses', 'Tithonus', 'St Simeon Stylites', 'The Lotos-Eaters', and in many of the sections of *In Memoriam*, such as 34 (xxxiv). The 'Morte d'Arthur' (composed in 1833 or 1834, after Hallam's death, first published in 1842, and republished much later as 'The Passing of Arthur', last of the *Idylls of the King*) speaks of the king's death, or translation to the Celtic paradise of Avilion, after the destruction of the Order of the Round Table, which was 'an image of the mighty world'. This was the effective beginning of the *Idylls*, at which Tennyson worked intermittently for forty years, although 'Balin and Balan', the last-written of the twelve idylls, was not published until 1885. It is typical that what the *Idylls* move towards is death: the death of Arthur, and with it the ruin of civilisation. Tennyson's outlook on life became gloomier as he grew older, and he was inclined to feel that *In Memoriam* was too hopeful, 'more than I am myself'. The *Idylls of the King*, in fact, depict the collapse of Western civilisation. Like others, he felt that some great catastrophe was inevitable. W.B. Yeats's (1865–1939) 'The Second Coming' depicts the return of Christ as that of a monster, in this age when 'the best lack all conviction, while the worst / Are full of passionate intensity'. Yeats's lines may derive from a passage in Shelley's *Prometheus Unbound*, and there are indications that his monstrous beast has something to do with that line of Tennyson's, repeated in the *Idylls*, where Arthur looks forward to what is to come: 'the fear lest this my realm. . . . / Reel back into the beast, and be no more'.

During the last thirty years or so, critics have been divided about the nature of Tennyson's achievements in the *Idylls*. Some regard it as the greatest poem of Victorian England. Others regard it as vitiated by its language, and powerful only in intention, and intermittently in conception. Even though the mode of idyll has its own reasons, and must not be mistaken for diluted epic, there is little doubt that the archaising language of the *Idylls* often fails. It is likely that Tennyson was suffering from the effects of a divided purpose. Indeed the *Idylls* suffer from a fairly constant effect of a direct translation of concept into idyll. The best of them are probably 'Merlin and Vivien', in which Merlin, the great enchanter and poet, and the creative imagination of King Arthur's Camelot, allows himself to be destroyed by the corrupt Vivien; 'Balin and Balan', where, in yet another vision of suicide, the twin brothers Balin and Balan, representing respectively the darker passions, and the controlling reason, kill each other; and of course 'The Passing of Arthur', of the vintage of the early 1830s, and magnificently rehandled for its place in the scheme. 'The Holy Grail' is a fair example of the effect of translation that one finds. Here the beginnings of the final destruction of the Order are shown, in the coming of false asceticism arising from thwarted sexual passion. The idyll is a powerful psychological study of frustration, and false penance. Or rather, it contains such a study. Yet although the structure is skilful, and the visionary poetry impressive, the reader is often conscious of being advised, even of being gently nudged into the best place to stand, if he is to get the full effect. The poetry is, as it were, on display. Many of Tennyson's contemporary readers had strong reservations about the *Idylls*, and some of them are among the best critics of Tennyson's poetry that we are likely to have. It must be admitted that some of the delighted and careful analysis of the *Idylls* that has gone on in the last thirty years or so, shrewd though much of it is, suggests, more than anything else, the workings of an academic industry, and the desire of academics (or some academics) to find something to write about. It has had some of the effects of an industry, for which 'Excalibur Enterprises' might be an appropriate name.

T.S. Eliot aptly remarked: 'Tennyson, who might unquestionably have been a consummate master of minor forms, took to turning out large patterns on a machine'. By 'minor forms' Eliot meant more than the short poem. But we should remember that Tennyson never lost his mastery of the short poem. The elegies, '"Frater Ave atque Vale"' (1883) and 'In the Garden at Swainston' (1874), and the celebratory 'To Virgil' (1882), where Tennyson praises the great Roman poet he admired so much, are among the finest of their kind. Elegiac though the first two are, they are instinct with life. This is a surprising feature of many of the later short poems. 'In the Garden at Swainston', on the death of his friend Sir John Simeon, speaks of death, but its dactylic rhythms, grave though they are, are not funereal.

Nightingales sang in his woods:
   The Master was far away:
Nightingales warbled and sang
   Of a passion that lasts but a day;
   Still in the house in his coffin the Prince of courtesy lay.

Two dead men have I known
   In courtesy like to thee:
Two dead men have I loved
   With a love that ever will be:
   Three dead men have I loved and thou art last of the three.

The pulse of life is clearly felt in the fine poems of social converse, such as to 'To E. Fitzgerald' (1885), 'To Mary Boyle' (1889), even in 'To the Marquis of Dufferin and Ava' (1889), written on the death abroad of his son Lionel. Their mode is classical. They derive from, and adorn, a long tradition of highly cultivated European poetry, whose starting point is friendship among equals, and the maintenance of civilised values. As such, they may be called aristocratic, in the only effective sense of the word. The idea of egalitarianism, the modern habit of regarding tradition as regressive, together with the assumption that what we should expect from poets is highly coloured individual experience, may make them even less popular than poetry usually is in England. Tennyson was uniquely qualified to write this kind of poetry. It is a pity he did not write more of it. Perhaps he lacked the necessary habit of serenity. On the other hand, it is probably wrong to speak of this as necessary, since what seem to be serenity and untroubled acceptance in poetry are often the products of minds in search of calm. Both intimate and public as they are – 'To the Marquis of Dufferin and Ava' is on the theme of public service, as well as grief, and the implication is of a society of equals, whether named or not – they represent a public side of Tennyson better than his laureate poems. Of these, only the 'Ode on the Death of the Duke of Wellington' is touched with greatness; there are fine passages, but there is also a fair amount of solemn lingering on the subject. As for the Romantic quest, and its expression in myth, 'Merlin and the Gleam', written three years before his death, in a mode deriving from old alliterative English poetry, is a late and poignant statement. Merlin is Tennyson, the artificer and enchanter. His task is to follow the gleam or magic light that leads onward.

And so to the land's
Last limit I came –
And can no longer,
But die rejoicing,
For through the Magic

Of Him the Mighty,
Who taught me in childhood,
There on the border
Of boundless Ocean,
And all but in Heaven
Hovers The Gleam

There are two references in the poem to the Wizard or Master who taught him in his childhood. Since no one master taught Tennyson, the reference is simply to the fact that magic and enchantment are the product of skill, and are handed on from one generation to the next. Wordsworth was the immediate English predecessor whom he most admired, and 'Merlin and the Gleam' is like a personal insistence on the great Romantic sense, as expressed by Wordsworth, of 'something evermore about to be', in l.608 of the sixth book of *The Prelude*. As such, it is something both a little more, and a little less than Wordsworth's concept, and may fittingly represent the tradition of English Victorian poetry.

The language of the poems

Tennysonian verse is sometimes thought to be synonymous with the slow-moving and the languorous, as in the Spenserian narrative stanzas of 'The Lotos-Eaters'. The pulse is often slow, and the language ornate, but the variety is such that 'Tennysonian' in this sense is very misleading. A glance at some of the sections of *Maud*, with their dramatic rapidity and informality, will make this clear. Significantly, the slow pace is sometimes that of the adjectives. In the line 'The level waste, the rounding gray' from 'Mariana', four of the six words are adjectives, or adjectival, 'gray', and even perhaps 'waste', being adjectives serving as nouns. Such an art of the adjective, which turns away from the verbs and nouns of the language of action, reflects the attempt by the single mind to find stability in apprehending what is given, what it sees.

The 1830 'Song: A spirit haunts the year's last hours' is an example of Tennyson's slowest and most subtly varied pace. The image is that of an unnamed autumn spirit, a combination of neurotic gardener and earth spirit, who is a projection of the near neurosis of the observer. There is no harvest, and no promise: unlike Keats's 'Ode to Autumn', this is a song of death, and of the death, one feels, of the soul.

A spirit haunts the year's last hours

Dwelling amid these yellowing bowers:

  To himself he talks;

For at eventide, listening earnestly,

At his work you may hear him sob and sigh

    In the walks;

    Earthward he boweth the heavy stalks

Of the mouldering flowers:

    Heavily hangs the broad sunflower

      Over its grave i' the earth so chilly;

    Heavily hangs the hollyhock,

    Heavily hangs the tiger-lily.

The stresses have been marked according to a simple pattern. (Variations in weight of stress marks, of from / to /////, or 5 to 1, are regarded by some scholars as essential; the only variation above is that of / or ᴗ. Incidentally, the first line may well gain from reading 'spirit' as a monosyllable – 'sprit' – as Tennyson sometimes pronounced it.

A sprit haunts the year's last hours

throws the weight of three uninterrupted strong stresses on the last three monosyllabic words, where it seems to belong. It is true that the verb 'haunts' would then become unstressed, as 'haunts,' and that this may seem a cavalier way of treating the first verb in the poem; on the other hand, 'spirit' (or 'sprit') already contains the sense of 'haunts'.) The rhythm is a mixture of dactylic (/ ᴗ ᴗ) and trochaic (/ ᴗ), with ana-crusis, or unstressed introductory syllables, in six of the first eight lines. At the same time, the first, third, and sixth lines sound iambic, and anapaestic. English dactyls and trochees often risk being taken over by iambs and anapaests, since the natural rhythm of English verse is a rising rhythm. The refrain of the last four lines, where there is no anacrusis, confirms the essentially falling rhythm throughout, following from line 7. The fact that there is no sense of change when we pass to the last four lines makes it clear what is happening. The verse demands very careful attention to weight, and pace. The first three lines are observations, culminating in the short 'To himself he talks,' which – partly because of the inversion, partly because of the unusual idea of a neurotic spirit that talks to itself – lingers over itself, in spite of its brevity, before the fourth and fifth lines, with the explicatory 'For', swell into what begins to seem the true pace of the poem, despite the anacrusis. The movement of the refrain is so slow that 'sunflower' sounds like 'sun flower,' so distinguishing between this and the 'flowers' of the preceding line, so that there is no danger of a false rhyme. It is as much the slow pace as the rhythm which gives the meaning: even to the sunflower.

Coleridge did not approve of the rhythms of some of the early poems, saying he could hardly scan them. He also suggested that Tennyson did not really know what metre was. Later in the nineteenth century a critic found the 'Song' 'ear-torturing', and metrically indefensible and unintelligible. There was at least no danger of this critic's thinking of the 'Song' as 'word-music', with which we tend to associate Tennyson, more perhaps than most poets. But a distinction must be made. Word-music is severely limited, since, apart from the obvious restrictions of tone, the meaning of the words is denotative as well as connotative, unlike notes in music, whose meaning is almost wholly connotative, and depends on their context. In an early poem such as 'Claribel' (1830), subtitled 'A Melody', Tennyson is experimenting with simple word music: 'The slumbrous wave outwelleth,/The babbling runnel crispeth,/The hollow grot replieth/Where Claribel low-lieth'. The limitations of this are more obvious than those of anything in the early unpublished 'Ilion, Ilion'.

Ilion, Ilion, dreamy Ilion, pillared Ilion, holy Ilion,
City of Ilion when wilt thou by melody born?
Blue Scamander, yellowing Simois from the heart of piny Ida
Everwhirling from the molten snows upon the mountainthrone,
Roll Scamander, ripple Simois, ever onward to a melody
Manycircled, overflowing thorough and thorough the flowery
    level of unbuilt Ilion,
City of Ilion, pillared Ilion, shadowy Ilion, holy Ilion,
    To a music merrily flowing, merrily echoing
    When wilt thou be melody born?

But this, significantly enough, is largely because of the sense: Tennyson speaks of the magical birth by melody, of which the city of Ilion or Troy, built by the music of the god Apollo, is a supreme example. He is wiser here than some other nineteenth-century poets, whose more experimental word music is a desperate response to the difficulty of establishing meaning in the modern world, by insisting on language wholly as charm, or spell. In 'Ilion, Ilion' the word music is subordinated to the myth.

Sometimes the onomatopoeia diverts our attention from more subtle effects.

    So saying, from the ruined shrine he stept
And in the moon athwart the place of tombs,
Where lay the mighty bones of ancient men,
Old knights, and over them the sea-wind sang
Shrill, chill, with flakes of foam.

This, from the 'Morte d'Arthur', culminates in the onomatopoeia of 'shrill, chill', and many readers do not look farther than this. Yet the passage is more complex. The 'Morte d'Arthur' shows a reduction of life from its ideal, to a bleak actuality, and the movement of this sentence, in which Sir Bedivere leaves the wounded and dying king, to go down to the lake, and throw away the magic sword Excalibur, is also in its way reductive. After 'stept', and the 'And' and swelling vowels of the second line, and in spite of the absence of a comma, we expect a further and more marked verbal action. We do not get it, 'lay' and 'sang' being subordinated to the place of tombs. The effect is that of the further action suggested by 'stept / And' being replaced by a minor and syntactically subordinate movement of feeling, a sort of undersong suddenly becoming the whole business of the period. This is part of a reduction of (and from) action which is the theme of the 'Morte d'Arthur', and of the *Idylls* as a whole. It occurs also in a vowel-meaning more subtle, though not in its way more effective, than the culminating vowel-music. 'Old knights' is brief, and parenthetical. It takes up what precedes it, reducing it to a passing word, or formality; at the same time, its vowels both shorten and reverse those of the heroic 'mighty bones'.

Although Tennyson can be ornate, his language is capable of great restraint. The 'Morte d'Arthur', a highly literary epic episode, is like a nineteenth-century dream of epic. (In some senses it is more of a dream of epic than Keats's *Hyperion*, with its broken armour and magic sword, in place of Keats's gods and temples.) It is not only the King who is lost, leaving Sir Bedivere, his last knight, to live on in a cold world without him. An age has been lost, an age of graciousness and high deeds. When Tennyson published it in 1842, he gave it a preface and epilogue which he called 'The Epic', in which the poem is read to his friends at Christmas by a frustrated poet, as the surviving book of his epic poem, destroyed because he thought it old-fashioned. So framed, the poem has the force of an act of despair, yet paradoxically is also something of an act of faith in poetry. We may feel that it insists a little too much on its bleakness, that the coldness and spareness invoked are those of a highly literary age, but if we compare it with the 'Sohrab and Rustum' (1853) of Matthew Arnold (1822–88), the differences are striking. Arnold's poem is a brief epic-style action, in which a father unknowingly kills his son. There is much less action in Tennyson's poem, yet literary though both poems are, there is little doubt which suffers more from an excess of epic trappings. In some respects, Arnold had aimed at a plain style. The historian James Froude (1818–94), indeed, pointed out that the word 'tent' occurs half a dozen times in the first eighteen lines of the poem, and suggested that Arnold 'had overdone the plainness of expression which he so much studies'. On the other hand, long epic or heroic similes abound in Arnold's poem; sometimes it seems that no sooner has one ended, than another begins. In the 'Morte d'Arthur', however, there are only three epic similes throughout, which hardly makes for decoration.

Sometimes it is the terms of an authoritative Tennysonian image which can be mistaken for decoration, as in this, from 'Tithonus':

> Can thy love,
> Thy beauty, make amends, though even now,
> Close over us, the silver star, thy guide,
> Shines in those tremulous eyes that fill with tears
> To hear me?

The withering Tithonus looks into the tear-filled eyes of the goddess Aurora, pleading to be allowed to die. Aurora weeps, but like Tithonus she is powerless. He sees his answer in the reflection in her eyes of the star of Venus. As goddess of generation, Venus has been slighted by his immortality, and his escape from the cycle of generation, and the pitiless answer to his pleading is there in the reflection of her silver star. The phrase 'the silver star' is exactly at the centre of the passage. This jewel-like intensity is very far from the ornate, or the self-indulgent.

There is a characteristic stillness about these two passages, from the 'Morte d'Arthur', and 'Tithonus'. Tennyson's movement can be rapid, not merely in *Maud*: the verse of 'The Lady of Shalott', despite a central stillness in the poem, is hardly slow. In 'Locksley Hall', the apparent forward-swinging movement expresses the struggling of indecision: the long trochaic lines beat out frustration, and that self-contempt which declares itself in contempt for others. His most characteristic movements, however, are the lingering of 'Mariana', which is implicit also in 'Ulysses'; the circling or cyclic movement of *In Memoriam*; and those movements of accretion and parallelism expressed by the use of 'and'. The quiet 'and's' of the passage quoted from the 'Morte d'Arthur' contribute to the process by which the inactive, and apparently minor, becomes a major principle: 'And in the moon ... and over them'. In 'To E. Fitzgerald', the 'and's' linger with the thought of death, like a pulse beating more and more slowly.

> Remembering all the golden hours
> Now silent, and so many dead,
> And him the last

'To E. Fitzgerald' is in fact like an exercise in the use of 'and', and many of the conjunctions in the single first period which makes up the first part of the poem begin lines, as if Tennyson wanted to emphasise this. Of course, it is a musing accretion of memories; this is how the poem proceeds, and that first long period is like a single line of life, unbroken, and rejoicing quietly in its fullness. The conjunctions in the second part of the poem, on Fitzgerald's death, echo, as one feels they must, those of the first part, with the shadow of the death behind them.

Among Tennyson's most skilful uses of accretion is the following, from 'Audley Court', which makes no use of conjunctions.

> So sang we each to either, Francis Hale,
> The farmer's son, who lived across the bay,
> My friend

These musing phrases follow each other very quietly; the pauses between them become longer and longer, leaving the brief 'my friend', on which they end, to return the glad present of the poem to the past, from which it was evoked. In section 87 (LXXXVII) of *In Memoriam*, there is an interesting variation in the use of 'and'. Tennyson revisits Cambridge after Hallam's death, and walks about the colleges and the town, reliving what he has known. Outside the door of what were Hallam's rooms at Trinity College he hears the loud noise of a wine party, and thinks, as he stands there, of the debates of the intellectual Apostles in that very room, when they hung on Hallam's words. During the first part of the poem, the 'and's' express the dream-like state of reliving the past in these familiar places.

> And heard once more in college fanes
>   The storm their high-built organs make,
>   And thunder-music, rolling, shake
> The prophet blazoned on the panes;
>
> And caught once more the distant shout,
>   The measured pulse of racing oars
>   Among the willows; paced the shores
> And many a bridge, and all about
>
> The same gray flats again, and felt
>   The same, but not the same; and last
>   Up that long walk of limes I past
> To see the rooms in which he dwelt.

(They are varied authoritatively by that single 'but': I 'felt / The same, but not the same.') In the last part, however, they are urgent and rapid, as they move to a living recollection of Hallam as he was, in his glory.

> Who, but hung to hear
> The rapt oration flowing free
>
> From point to point, with power and grace,
>   And music in the bounds of law,

To those conclusions when we saw
The God within him light his face,

And seem to lift the form, and glow
In azure orbits heavenly-wise;
And over these ethereal eyes
The bar of Michael Angelo.

(The last two lines refer to Hallam's claim to possess the prominent bar or ridge of bone over the eyes which the great Italian artist and poet Michael Angelo possessed, and which is sometimes thought to be a mark of unusual mental power.) Once again, and like the sixty-sixth sonnet of Shakespeare, the poem could be described as an exercise in 'and', an analogy with music which is more valid than most.

The great example of the cyclic movement is, of course, *In Memoriam*, as in the *abba* stanza which is its basic mode. The *aa* rhyme returns the fourth line to the first, after a separating *bb* couplet; the effect is to leave something of both rhymes, so to speak, in the air, the *bb* rhyme being in part superseded, the *aa* rhyme dispersed. The use of it by other poets shows how Tennyson's mastery of it is peculiarly his own.

Fantastic grow the evening-gowns.
Agents of the Fisc pursue
Absconding tax-defaulters through
The sewers of provincial towns.

This, from 'The Fall of Rome', by the modern English poet W.H. Auden (1907–73), is excellent, but it is hard to realise that it is in the same measure as *In Memoriam*. The gravity, the slow parallel movements, the circling, are all absent, despite the rhymes. Tennyson sometimes used the measure elsewhere, as in the epistolary poem 'To E.L., on His Travels in Greece'. The structure of this poem is as cyclic as its stanza. The two sentences that make up the poem begin and end with scenes that Edward Lear (1812–88), painter and writer of nonsense verse, had drawn in Greece, and the verbs ending the first sentence and beginning the second sentence act at the heart of the poem as the equivalent of a *bb* structure.

The technical expertise of *Maud* is, as has been suggested in Part 2, not merely a matter of different modes for each section. The sonnet form of I, iii, and the reasons for it, have been discussed briefly there. Perhaps one could add, that the reason why Tennyson chose the sonnet form for this section is that the hero is faced with a new and disturbing experience, which has to be grappled with, and held in the mind as an entirety, so that it can be understood. For such an effect, the sonnet form, with its complex rhymes, and above all its impression of an integral whole, is pre-eminently suitable. This is an example of a master of his craft turning to a classic form as the perfect expression of an experience. The form of I, xxii, on the other hand, with its sudden reversal in the last stanza, is his own invention: so much part of the stage in the drama which he has reached, that it would be inappropriate to think of it in any other context. The repetitions in the six- or eight-line stanzas of the poem are such that they seem to run or dance from the opening phrase, usually ending on a recapitulative repetition, which serves as a kind of refrain. The last stanza, however, begins by recapitulating a phrase from the stanza before it, and the stanza does not seem to begin until its second line, which, instead of repeating what has gone before, introduces what is to come. 'She is coming, my own, my sweet' repeats the third and fourth lines of the preceding stanza, and is not itself repeated, an effect which, by this time, one has learned to expect in the poem.

> Were it ever so airy a tread,
> My heart would hear her and beat
> Were it earth in an earthy bed;
> My dust would hear her and beat,
> Had I lain for a century dead;
> Would start and tremble under her feet,
> And blossom in purple and red.

The effect is to cause a sudden rising movement, appropriate to the ecstasy before the catastrophe. The virtuosity of *Maud*, of course, makes it almost unique in Tennyson.

Elsewhere his own moods are sometimes conveyed by the simpler movements of fine rhetoric, as in 'Vastness' (1885), with its grim indictment of a meaningless world, turning at the end to the love which gives it meaning.

> Trade flying over a thousand seas with her spice
>   and her vintage, her silk and her corn;
> Desolate offing, sailorless harbours, famishing populace,
>   wharves forlorn . . .

> Wealth with his wines and his wedded harlots;
>   honest Poverty, bare to the bone;
> Opulent Avarice, lean as Poverty; Flattery gilding
>   the rift in a throne . . .

> What is it all, if we all of us end but in being our own
>   corpse-coffins at last,
> Swallowed in Vastness, lost in Silence, drowned
>   in the deeps of a meaningless Past?

> What but a murmur of gnats in the gloom,
> or a moment's anger of bees in their hive? –
>
>   *   *   *   *
>
> Peace, let it be! for I loved him, and love him for ever:
> the dead are not dead but alive.

Simpler modulations than some of the others, perhaps, though it may take a little time and effort to appreciate the force of that powerful falling rhythm, with its hesitations, and strong confirmations. But simple only in the best and plainest sense, in what Tennyson does with the reversal of the last line. It seems longer, because of its monosyllables, which expand, as monosyllables will do in such a line. Because of its form, as well as the dramatic reversal which it states, the line challenges all that has gone before; it has the simplicity of a defiant gesture.

He is one of the most literary of poets. This, together with the fact that he seems to have had few intellectual ambitions other than in poetry, has made some readers suspect his seriousness of purpose. But the accusation of literariness – for it is often used as an accusation – should be treated with caution. Poets have always drawn on their predecessors, and we must not allow our understanding of this to be clouded by sentimental ideas about originality, purity of inspiration, and so forth. The echoes of other poets which we find in Tennyson testify, here as elsewhere, to the authority of that old tradition, of the continual creation by all poets of the one great world poem. Like his English predecessors, he takes from, and recreates, Greek and Latin poets, such as Homer, Theocritus, Virgil, and Horace. He also draws freely on the great English tradition of Shakespeare, and Milton. *The Princess*, his Victorian narrative comedy, is full of Shakespearean verse and image.

>   loose
> A flying charm of blushes o'er this cheek,
> Where they like swallows coming out of time
> Will wonder why they came

The pace and imagery of this are unmistakably Shakespearean. The simile of vii, ll.147–54, where the yielding Ida is compared to Aphrodite or Venus ('lovelier in her mood / Than in her mould that other') is Miltonic. It is a tradition in which he has an honoured place, because of what he gave it.

Part 4

Hints for study

THE FOLLOWING NOTES are designed to help you to study Tennyson's poetry, and to write coherently about it. There is no substitute for close study of the poems, and for readiness to examine every possibility, without fantasy or exaggeration. Poetry is simple, in the sense that it is an organic whole. In most other respects it is highly complex. The combination of simplicity and complexity is one of the reasons why its study is so rewarding. The study of poetry has to be taken seriously. If you learn to parrot a large number of phrases in selected contexts, and if your examiners are careless, you may, with luck, manage to scrape through an examination. But you will have learned nothing.

Answers, or material for answers, are provided for some of the questions which follow (pp. 74–9). For others, a few suggestions only are given.

Quotation

The strongly physical nature of poetry makes it easy to memorise, and you should take advantage of this. But although it is most useful to learn passages of poetry, you should avoid offering too many long quotations in essays and examination answers. There are few more boring essays for an examiner to read, than the essay which consists basically of a thin trickle of critical comment leading from one long quotation to the next. Remember that real *knowledge and perception* are of the greatest importance; that this should be articulated in a logical and coherent *argument*, and that quotation should be *to the point*. It should make the reader think: 'yes, exactly – that is how it is'. It should never resemble a vague gesture in the general direction of the argument. Suppose, for example, you are discussing the fifty-sixth section of *In Memoriam*, and want to make it clear by quotation what Tennyson feels man is, and whether his only future is to disappear, like so many other types of life. If you were to say 'for Tennyson, if man is a type of life which Nature may destroy, he is "a monster," an aberration', you would be making your point authoritatively, and with that necessary minimum of quotation ('a monster') which shows that you mean business. A more extended quotation is sometimes convenient, and sometimes necessary, but you should try to cultivate the habit of brief reference. Like other habits, it forms the mind. You will soon find yourself thinking more clearly as a result, and writing nearer to the point.

What to look for

For critics as for poets, there is no substitute for the excitement in the language itself. Without that, there is nothing. There may be all sorts of reasons why it need not be so; the fact is, that it is so. Never read poetry as if it were merely a translation of ideas into language. In an important sense, it is that. But if you forget the language, and read it for the sake of an abstraction to be called 'the ideas', 'the content', 'the message', you will learn nothing that could not be more conveniently learned in another medium.

Language is abused and cheapened by daily use. It has been well said of poetry, that its task is to take the whore language, and make a virgin of it. And if you are ever tempted to feel that language is merely the dress of thought, remember Shelley's lines from *Prometheus Unbound*, about how Prometheus 'gave man speech, and speech created thought, / Which is the measure of the universe'. You cannot think without language; it is language which to a large extent makes thought.

Of course, the historical and social contexts are important, as you will have understood by now. But there is little point in taking poetry merely as an illustration of social and historical processes. Its permanence is in its mode, which is language. The act of poetic creation begins in linguistic excitement; the act of critical perception, of the reader who apprehends, frequently ends in it, and in the consciousness that there is something there which defies analysis.

If English is a foreign language for you, this makes your task more difficult. The more you read, and the more closely you read, the more frequent become the moments of imaginative understanding. The experience of reading poetry in your own language is probably the most valuable preparation of all. Much depends on your culture. In England, the virtual national triumph of 'the plain blunt man' who cannot 'trouble his head over that sort of thing', and who prefers sociology, has done great damage. My own experience in teaching Arabic-speaking students has been rewardingly different.

Once you are clear about the historical and social context of the poem – and remember that the most important historical context is that of *mind* – study the language and imagery closely. Observe the rhythm and the word order: why is the order reversed in this phrase; what is the reason for the pause after that phrase; why does the rhythm change here, and when, and why, does it return to the first rhythm? What is the form, the almost physical shape, of the poem, and why does it have that shape? It has been said that a poem is an image of a mental process. What is the process in the poem you are studying, and how is it achieved? Is anything left open at the end? Is there any unanswered question, which perhaps cannot be answered, left hanging in the air, just off the end of the poem? Is there anything in the poem which seems to work, perhaps unconsciously, against what the poet seems to want to say?

You cannot understand the poem, of course, unless you understand something of the poet's intentions, and for that it is vital to recognise the type of poem that it is: ode, lyric, or dramatic monologue. Intentions are not always easily understood. Wordsworth's poem 'The Thorn', published with *Lyrical Ballads* in 1798, was something of a challenge to the educated public, like others of these poems. The tale of an unfortunate woman who might or might not have murdered her baby is told by a gossiping man with time on his hands, who questions the neighbours. It contains the apparently extraordinary couplet, about the sinister little pond:

I've measured it from side to side:
'Tis three feet long, and two feet wide.

Many readers made fun of these lines, and Wordsworth later changed them. Yet to squat down with a tape-measure and measure the pond is exactly what such a man would do, and behind the fussy statement is the suggestion, all the more grim for the banality that half conceals it, that there may well be some truth in the strange story, because the pond is a convenient size to drown a baby in. This, with the character of the narrator (which Wordsworth did not make sufficiently clear in the poem), is the context, and it is the context which gives the meaning. Elsewhere Wordsworth's directions can be clear enough. Towards the end of 'Simon Lee', also in *Lyrical Ballads*, he turns to reproach, even to mock his 'gentle' (that is, educated) reader, saying he fears that he will have been expecting a tale, and will be disappointed by this rambling and apparently pointless poem:

It is no tale; but, should you think,
Perhaps a tale you'll make it.

That 'should you think' and 'perhaps' express a strong contempt for the merely educated, who will not reach out, and understand.

How does one recognise great poetry? In one sense, it is a strange question. But after so much advice and exhortation, it may be entirely natural to ask it. Many readers have found that moments of imaginative, even creative understanding are accompanied by some degree of physical excitement. It is certainly not a matter of an approval of high moral sentiments sonorously expressed. Tennyson's dramatic monologue 'Tiresias' expresses high moral sentiments sonorously enough, but though he approved of the blank verse, it is a still and largely unrewarding poem. Whatever recognition there is can be guaranteed only by the strong sense of rhythm and shape; most of all, perhaps, by the feeling that the words have been recreated, and that you are seeing and hearing them for the first time. Beyond that, it tends to be a matter of the opposition of great forces, and the tensions which result from this.

Questions

Of the specimen questions that follow, the first is fully answered, and may be used as a model. Some of the material for answers to questions 2 and 3 is given, and it would be a useful exercise to arrange what is given into coherent answers. The remaining three questions are each followed by a brief note of how they might be answered.

In arranging your material, you may find it useful to number your notes, with cross-references when two or more topics seem to be closely connected. It should then be possible, after careful examination of your notes, to work out a coherent scheme. But there is one danger in particular in this, which is that you may be tempted to set out your scheme too quickly, in the form of a neat list of speciously reassuring numbers, without having properly considered whether it represents a logical argument, or a string of mere associations. Orators used to be praised for 'the justness of their transitions', or their manner of passing from point to point, and Thomas De Quincey (1785–1859) speaks highly of Coleridge's transitions in discourse. (Tennyson himself, in a passage from *In Memoriam* 87 (LXXXVII), quoted in Part 3, speaks of Hallam's 'rapt oration flowing free / From point to point,' and speaks too of its music being 'in the bounds of law'.) The steps of your argument must be made plain by proper transitions. With a little practice, you will soon recognise when you are deceiving your reader (and yourself), and will be able to correct yourself, and form proper habits. The teachers of our childhood, after all, were right: there is a difference between 'and' and 'but'. A loosely associated group of ideas is not enough; leave accretion to Tennyson, whose logic is poetic logic, and make your argument coherent.

---

(1) Consider what part the three voices play in 'The Golden Year'.

The question seems to refer to the voice of the poet Leonard, and the voice of Old James, together with the blast from the slate quarry, which, though not a human voice, is produced by men, and ends the poem by seeming to comment on what has been said. There is, of course, a fourth voice, which is that of the narrator. It is this voice which presents the context, and interprets the action. Of the three other voices, those of Leonard and James offer opposing points of view. The blast from the quarry is an oblique yet authoritative comment on this opposition, and indeed on language itself.

'The Golden Year' is in the tradition of the 'English Idyls'. Like many of them, it deals with contemporary life. Its mode, or method, derives from the Theocritean idyll, which offered a small picture or image of the complexities of a modern age, and which sometimes included a song contest. In place of songs by two shepherds, Tennyson gives us the song of the poet Leonard, and the angry and contemptuous rebuttal by old James. Leonard is probably a half-mocking self-portrait by Tennyson. He is uncertain about man's future, and about the place of poetry in the modern world. He wistfully recalls old dreams of the coming golden year, or golden age, when man would be prosperous, and at peace, and is silent before the remonstrances of James. James's remarks are to be take as prose, against Leonard's song. This is a modern contest, and Leonard, the poet, is on his own, speaking in figures to a world which hardly understands him. The model for James is probably Thomas Carlyle (1795–1881), the brilliant, gloomy, and sometimes explosive nineteenth-century Scottish historian and political philosopher. James's gospel of work is very much that of mid-nineteenth-century England. At its worst, it led to a glorification of material prosperity – which Carlyle abominated and of course the ethic of work for the sake of work is open to many abuses. Here it reflects a passionate desire on the part of James to get rid of nonsense, and to see things as they are: man was not born to be idle; progress is possible, and we must work for it; hope is kept alive in 'him who works, and feels he works'.

In one sense, the opposition between Leonard and James is a matter of time. To James, the future that the poet celebrates is 'like the second world to us that live', so far away it is. Leonard, too, like Tennyson himself, is oppressed by time: 'But we grow old'. Perhaps this is why he looks to an idealised process of time, by which the golden year will surely come. But it is not a matter of a simple opposition between the two. For the modern age, neither Leonard's images, nor James's gospel of work seem adequate. Each in its different way is an avoidance of reality. The sense of wordless processes which are beginning to direct man is evident in the blast from the quarry which follows James's outburst. It seems to complete James's remarks: this is the work he speaks of. But in another way it makes nonsense of them: would these workers feel, with him, that the golden year 'is ever at the doors'? And in yet another sense, the wordless blast and its dramatic echoes counter the language of both song and speech, a sardonic comment on both.

---

(2) Is the speaker in 'Ulysses' presented as a heroic or unheroic figure?

In any discussion of a poem the poet's intentions must be kept in mind. But with 'Ulysses', we tend to be stopped at once, since we are not sure of Tennyson's intentions. The mode may not help us very much: it is that of dramatic monologue, and we are accustomed to thinking of dramatic monologue as a form in which it often happens that the speaker tells us more about himself than he is conscious of. This question often occurs in examination papers, because there has been so much discussion among critics about it. Some help, but not, perhaps, very much, can be found in Tennyson's comments on it. He remarked that the poem, written after Hallam's death, under a sense of great loss, gives the feeling of going forward and braving the struggle of life, and also that it was written under the sense that (in spite of everything) life must be fought out to the end. The need to fight it out to the end probably expresses his sense more completely than the need to go forward. Ulysses is weakened by age, as Tennyson is by grief, but there will be no yielding. To that extent, the poem celebrates will, as does *In Memoriam*.

Against this, it has been argued that the language of the poem is elegiac rather than heroic, and also that Ulysses, after all, abandons his aged wife, and his Ithacan subjects. It has also been argued that in the third paragraph, where he hands over his duties to his son Telemachus, he seems to speak of him with something like contempt, as of a lesser man fit to undertake an unheroic task, that of civilising the savage Ithacans. (We now know, from the manuscript drafts of the poem, that he does not show contempt.) One critic has gone so far as to argue that Tennyson presents Ulysses as an example of arrogance, and selfishness. Whether or not Tennyson presents Ulysses as noble seems therefore to be a puzzling question. We should remember, perhaps, that he took the idea of the last voyage for the Greek hero from the great Italian poet Dante, who tells how Ulysses insisted on voyaging farther than man should, in pursuit of knowledge, and how he was punished for it by God, and suffered in Hell. At the same time, there is no clear evidence that Tennyson is using Ulysses as a type of searcher after forbidden knowledge. The question of what might and might not be permitted to man had changed somewhat since Dante's day, and a man of Tennyson's age would view a Romantic quest rather differently.

As for the language, it is obviously slow-moving, and sometimes elegiac in tone:

The long day wanes: the slow moon climbs: the deep
Moans round with many voices.

Does this mean that it is unheroic? What is heroic language for one age may not be recognisably heroic for another. The apparent dismissal of his aged wife Penelope, who had remained faithful to Ulysses during his long absence, is difficult to reconcile with nobility, or heroism. Perhaps Tennyson is taking advantage of the idea of another age, with other ideas of conduct. On the other hand, although Ulysses intends to leave, is he brutally dismissing Penelope, as some critics have thought? 'Matched with an agèd wife': it is uncompromising enough, but it is probably meditation, not speech to Penelope. For all we know to the contrary, this Penelope might have approved of an appropriately heroic death for her husband. As for the characterisation of Telemachus, we must remember that words like 'prudent', 'useful', 'blameless', and 'decent', though hardly Romantic, are not condescending. They indicate high attributes, not limitations.

Perhaps the best thing to bear in mind is the idea of not yielding to a life of desolate commonplace which threatens to destroy you. It is likely that this must override most other considerations. One thing which is clear is that the poem is of an unusual complexity, and that no easy decisions about it are possible.

---

(3) Discuss Lancelot's rôle in 'The Lady of Shalott'.

Lancelot appears twice in 'The Lady of Shalott'. His first dramatic appearance, and its effect on the Lady, is described at length in Part III, and at the end of the poem it is he who prays for her when she is dead. The Lady seems to represent the withdrawn spirit of the artist, who is destroyed if he meets the world directly on its own terms. This is why she weaves alone in her island tower, symbol of her isolation. She must not stop, or look down the river to Camelot, which symbolises the life of the world. Her only sight of life is in her mirror, in which 'Shadows of the world appear'.

Lancelot, on the other hand, is a male principle, representing action. He is the greatest knight of Camelot, and he is also the guilty lover of Queen Guinevere. When he appears, it is at the time of harvest and fruition, from which the Lady is apart. (Since he is unmarried, and his love for the Queen is adulterous, it could be said that he too stands apart from these processes, however splendid his appearance and prowess.) 'A bow-shot from her bower-eaves, / He rode between the barley-sheaves': bow-shot, the physical action, works against the sheltered and sheltering feminine bower. The strong b-sounds at the beginning mark Lancelot's sudden entry into the Lady's world. The stanzas which describe him are full of light and sound: the sun flames on his greaves; his shield sparkles, his bridle and thick-jewelled saddle-leather glitter and shine; his helmet, helmet-feather, and brow burn and glow;

he sings as he goes, and his bridle-bells and armour ring. Light, sound, and the mastery of the warrior and horseman break in upon the still world of the Lady, and she leaves her web, and looks down to Camelot.

At the end of the poem, Lancelot seems like another man. The Lady's death has seemingly changed the world, and is now part of the approaching winter season. Camelot is hushed, and so is Lancelot, musing quietly on her death. It seems to be the first time he has seen her; nothing in the poem suggests that he saw her look down from her tower. He is different from the others who come out to look at the strange boat, with the dead Lady on it, not only because he is the greatest knight of them all, but because of what he knows of guilt, and human weakness. It seems that Lancelot is no longer the magnificent figure of Part III, who irresistibly drew the Lady to look from her tower, and leave her tapestry. He is human now in another sense: that is, in his understanding, and charity. There is a moving inconsequence in what he says: 'She has a lovely face; / God in his mercy lend her grace'. The apparent illogicality of this is very human, as is the resolution of it all in prayer.

---

(4) Discuss the methods by which Tennyson presents a state of desolation in 'Mariana'.

Your answer should contain a good deal about the language and versification of the poem. The one repeated cry in the refrain, with its few but powerful variations; the relative lack of strong enjambment or run-on in the lines, so that they seem to fall with a soft even pace; the constant circling and return in the *abbacddc* rhyme of the body of the stanza: these could usefully be discussed. Note the force of the enjambment in ll.76−7, and the very different effect of that of ll.28−9, which is neutralised by the passivity implicit in 'Came to her'. The nature of the few other living things in the poem should also be considered. Observe also the dream-like sequence of night and day in the stanzas; work out what time each stanza deals with, and the symmetry or form of this in the poem as a whole. Consider also in what ways the last two stanzas represent a climax to this desolation.

---

(5) Discuss the variety of Tennyson's poetry.

The difficulty with this question is that, without appearing to do so, it may ask more than you can give, since by implication it is comparative. If you answer it by pointing to instances of variety in Tennyson's poetry, you are still left with the unspoken question, how much variety is there in him compared with other poets? You may not find it easy to answer this, however briefly. Variety of mode is not difficult to illustrate: satire, elegy, lyric, idyll. Technical variety is an obvious matter for discussion: *Maud* is clearly one text to be discussed here. You might find it useful to speak also of monotony, and *In Memoriam* could be discussed from this angle. You might also have a good deal to say about a lack of variety in theme: the constant theme of loss, and frustration, for example. How important is this, compared with variety in the verse forms?

---

(6) Consider the importance of the will in Tennyson's poetry.

For most readers, will is important in Tennyson's poetry. Not surprisingly, spiritual stagnation of one sort or another matters too, as in 'Mariana' and 'The Lotos-Eaters'. This could be a useful question for you, since it illustrates the need to understand the context of any statement, and to remember possible corollaries or inferences. You must stick to the question: agreed, but you must also get that question (if only briefly) in its proper context. One poem which should be considered is *In Memoriam*, and the stubborn human struggle against despair, as well as the consonance of human and divine will towards the end. Another is 'Ulysses' and you might find it useful to consider how far the elegiac note of the verse implies spiritual stagnation. There is the will to death at the beginning and end of *Maud*, and between them the surrender to happiness, with the decision also to live a life of truth. There is the neurotic will to self-destruction and sainthood in 'St Simeon Stylites'. In 'The Golden Year' there is the yearning of Leonard towards, and his wistful invocation of, a great will in mankind which is plainly not his, over against the strong if limited will of James. How far the circumstances of Tennyson's age contribute to this insistence on individual will is a question worth following up. The poem 'Will' (1855) should also be studied.

Part 5

Suggestions for further reading

The text

The standard modern edition is that by Christopher Ricks, *The Poems of Tennyson*, Longman's Annotated English Poets, Longman, London, 1969, which omits the plays. The complete edition of the *Works* by Hallam Tennyson, Eversley Edition, Macmillan, London, 1907–8, 9 vols., may be consulted. The one-volume *Works*, Macmillan, London, 1913, is also useful. The best of the selections are those edited by Michael Millgate, *Tennyson: Selected Poems*, New Oxford English Series, Oxford University Press, Oxford, 1963, and John D. Jump, *'In Memoriam', 'Maud' and Other Poems*, Dent, London, 1975.

Biography

Hallam Tennyson's *Alfred, Lord Tennyson: a Memoir*, Macmillan, London, 2 vols, 1897 (usually described as the *Memoir*) contains a fascinating biographical record. *Tennyson and His Friends*, also edited by Hallam Tennyson, Macmillan, London, 1911, is also of interest.

More recent biographical studies are those by Sir Charles Tennyson, and Robert Bernard Martin. Sir Charles Tennyson, *Alfred Tennyson*, Macmillan, London, 1950, provided a great deal of new information, together with much shrewd interpretation. The standard biography now is that of Robert Bernard Martin, *Tennyson: The Unquiet Heart*, Faber and Faber, London, 1980. Some of the critical arguments about the poetry are uncertain, but as biography it is detailed, and sound.

Criticism

BUCKLEY, J.H. *Tennyson: The Growth of a Poet*, Harvard University Press, Cambridge, Mass., 1960.

CULLER, A. DWIGHT, *The Poetry of Tennyson*, Yale University Press, New Haven and London, 1977.

HUNT, JOHN DIXON, (ED.), *Tennyson: In Memoriam*, (Casebook Series) Macmillan, London, 1970.

JUMP, JOHN D. (ED.), *Tennyson: The Critical Heritage*, Routledge, London, 1967.

KILLHAM, JOHN (ED.), *Critical Essays on the Poetry of Tennyson*, Routledge, London, 1960.

PRIESTLEY, F.E.L.: *Language and Structure in Tennyson's Poetry*, Deutsch, London, 1973.

RICKS, CHRISTOPHER, *Tennyson*, Macmillan, New York, 1972.

The best of these is probably Ricks's *Tennyson*. The anthology edited by Jump includes a good deal of valuable contemporary criticism.

The author of these notes

Alastair Thomson, a graduate of the University of Edinburgh, is Professor of English at the New University of Ulster. He has taught at universities in Iraq, the Sudan, and Nigeria (where he was Professor at the University of Ibadan), as well as in England and Ireland. His publications include *Valéry* (1965), and an anthology of critical essays on Wordsworth, *Wordsworth's Mind and Art* (1969), and he contributed an essay on Tennyson ('Tennyson and Some Doubts') to *Essays & Studies 1982: The Poet's Power*.

The first 200 titles

Series number

BEN JONSON	*The Alchemist*	(102)
	Volpone	(15)
RUDYARD KIPLING	*Kim*	(114)
D. H. LAWRENCE	*Sons and Lovers*	(24)
	The Rainbow	(59)
	Women in Love	(143)
CAMARA LAYE	*L'Enfant Noir*	(191)
HARPER LEE	*To Kill a Mocking-Bird*	(125)
LAURIE LEE	*Cider with Rosie*	(186)
THOMAS MANN	*Tonio Kröger*	(168)
CHRISTOPHER MARLOWE	*Doctor Faustus*	(127)
	Edward II	(166)
SOMERSET MAUGHAM	*Of Human Bondage*	(185)
	Selected Short Stories	(38)
HERMAN MELVILLE	*Billy Budd*	(10)
	Moby Dick	(126)
ARTHUR MILLER	*Death of a Salesman*	(32)
	The Crucible	(3)
JOHN MILTON	*Paradise Lost I & II*	(94)
	Paradise Lost IV & IX	(87)
	Selected Poems	(177)
V. S. NAIPAUL	*A House for Mr Biswas*	(180)
SEAN O'CASEY	*Juno and the Paycock*	(112)
	The Shadow of a Gunman	(200)
GABRIEL OKARA	*The Voice*	(157)
EUGENE O'NEILL	*Mourning Becomes Electra*	(130)
GEORGE ORWELL	*Animal Farm*	(37)
	Nineteen Eighty-four	(67)
JOHN OSBORNE	*Look Back in Anger*	(128)
HAROLD PINTER	*The Birthday Party*	(25)
	The Caretaker	(106)
ALEXANDER POPE	*Selected Poems*	(194)
THOMAS PYNCHON	*The Crying of Lot 49*	(148)
SIR WALTER SCOTT	*Ivanhoe*	(58)
	Quentin Durward	(54)
	The Heart of Midlothian	(141)
	Waverley	(122)
PETER SHAFFER	*The Royal Hunt of the Sun*	(170)
WILLIAM SHAKESPEARE	*A Midsummer Night's Dream*	(26)
	Antony and Cleopatra	(82)
	As You Like It	(108)
	Coriolanus	(35)
	Cymbeline	(93)
	Hamlet	(84)
	Henry IV Part I	(83)
	Henry IV Part II	(140)
	Henry V	(40)
	Julius Caesar	(13)
	King Lear	(18)
	Love's Labour's Lost	(72)
	Macbeth	(4)
	Measure for Measure	(33)
	Much Ado About Nothing	(73)